THE OVERCOMERS' HANDBOOK OF KINGDOM PROCLAMATIONS

By

Barbara Potts

The author would like to acknowledge and thank McDougal Publishing for their work in typesetting and preparing this book for printing.

Kingdom Rising is a triune ministry of teaching, writing, and intercession dedicated to advancing the Kingdom of God in the earth through equipping and empowering believers in biblical principles of personal faith and spiritual warfare.

Published by:

Kingdom Rising Ministries

www.prayingwithpower.com

To contact the author:

blpotts@comcast.net

ISBN 978-1-58158-199-7

Printed in the United State of America
For Worldwide Distribution

CONTENTS

INTRODUCTION

I have been "praying the Word" and writing scriptural prayers and proclamations for about 17 years. I have shared the fruit of my prayer journey in my book, *Praying with Authority and Power*, first published in 2004. And while that was a *teaching* manual on spiritual warfare, this volume is a *prayer resource* tool, containing a collection of 77 of my proclamations and prayers on a variety of subjects. A recent statement by Graham Cooke particularly inspired me to follow the Lord's lead in this project:

**"We are in a time of Proclamation—
Crafted prayers empower overcoming."**

Jesus instructed us in Matthew 6:10 to pray that His Kingdom would come and His will be done on earth as it is in Heaven. I have a personal daily declaration I use in my devotions which says: "LORD, let Your Kingdom come and Your will be done in my life as in Heaven. *Revealing* Your Kingdom is my *priority. Fulfilling my assignment* in Your Kingdom is my *pleasure. Equipping* the Church to become Kingdom advancers is my *Passion!*"

So, my dear friends, it is my passionate prayer that this handbook of proclamations will help equip you as *overcoming warriors* who will advance His Kingdom on earth as it has already been established in Heaven!

*To him who **overcomes** I will grant to sit with Me on My throne ... .*

Revelation 3:21

Yours, O LORD, is the greatness,
The power and the glory,
The victory and the majesty;
For all that is in heaven and in earth is Yours;
Yours is the kingdom, O LORD,
And You are exalted as head over all.

1 Chronicles 29:11

CHAPTER 1

NATIONAL

CALLING FORTH AMERICA'S PROPHETIC DESTINY

As God's Kingdom people, we embrace the call of God's heart for our nation. We declare that God desires to bless us *so that we can fulfill our prophetic destiny as a Light Bearer and to bring the Gospel to the nations.*

And so we **arise and contend,** and we call forth the God-ordained prophetic destiny of this nation to be a *light of hope shining to the nations of the world.* We call forth the gates of our cities and nation to *be opened to the King of Glory, so that* His Kingdom can come and His will be done on earth as it has already been established in Heaven! *For…*

> *Yours, O Lord, is the greatness,*
> *The power and the glory,*
> *The victory and the majesty;*
> *For all that is in heaven and in earth is Yours;*
> *Yours is the kingdom, O Lord,*
> *And You are exalted as head over all.*   1 Chronicles 29:11

IT IS WRITTEN that the earth is the Lord's and all its fullness and all those who dwell therein. And the Lord sits as King forever (Psalm 24:1, 29)! Therefore, we proclaim that Jesus Christ is King and Lord over the United States of Christ. His power is supreme and His reign is eternal; and He alone shall be worshiped across our land.

And so we decree a release of God's glory to sweep across all seven mountains of society: the Church, the family, government, business and finance, education, media and technology and arts and entertainment. We declare that old wineskins are being broken in church and government structures. Cold coals of revival fire and dry wells of awakening are being stirred, re-fired and re-opened. We call forth the new wine and a fresh fire of Revival and Reformation that will invade and rebuild our culture.

We declare Kingdom culture and Kingdom alignment over our nation! We proclaim, from Isaiah 33:22:

The victory of justice over lawlessness ("For **the Lord** is our **Judge, ...**")

The authority of God's Law across our land (For **"the Lord** is our **Lawgiver, ..."**)

The majesty and Lordship of Jesus our King (For "**the Lord** is our **King, ..."**)

He will save us!

MIGHTY GOD, ESTABLISH THE DOMINION OF YOUR THRONE OVER OUR NATION!

KINGDOM FAITH PROCLAMATION
(DECLARING THE DOMINION OF HIS THRONE)

IT IS WRITTEN that the earth is the Lord's and all its fullness, and the Lord sits as King FOREVER (Psalm 24:1 and 29:10)! Therefore, we declare the Dominion of HIS Throne over our nation: *Jesus Christ is King and Lord over the United States of Christ.* His power is supreme and His reign is eternal. The Lion of Judah is roaring over the Church, our city and our nation, shaking and dismantling the anti-Christ, humanistic structure that has infected our government and society. Jesus is a fire around us and the glory in the midst of us (Hebrews 12:29, Isaiah 12:6). The Church is rising and shining with His Glory to dispel deep darkness from the people (Isaiah 60:1-2). Demonic strategies and terrorist attacks are being thwarted, deception exposed (Psalm 125:3), and the victory of the Lord is established through the power of His Blood and the Word of our testimony (Revelation 12:11). In the Name of Jesus, we overrule what satan has planned against God's land and God's people, and we cancel every demonic agenda, including the advancement of homosexuality, abortion, racism and sharia law. We declare that the BLOOD of Jesus has triumphed over and continues to prevail against these evil agendas and every demon associated with promoting them (Colossians 2:15).

We proclaim: Let GOD arise and His enemies be scattered (Psalm 68:1)! For the sake of our King and His Kingdom, we call forth the armies of heaven to engage in this battle and to encamp around and protect (Psalm 34:7) our borders, waterways, airways, highways, railways, subways, shipyards, military installations, government buildings, the power grid, cyberspace and all public venues, including schools, airports and airplanes, office buildings, shopping malls, post offices, movie theaters, hospitals, night clubs and churches.

For this purpose, the Son of God was made manifest: to destroy the works of the evil one (1 John 3:8). We proclaim that eviction notices have been served against the enemy of our souls and all of his demonic horde. By the order of Almighty God, he no longer has any authority over our families. He must cease and desist the actions, plans and lies he has perpetrated against them. We call the prodigals forth who are now set free from every bondage to return to their God! We decree that angels have been released to set up camp around our homes (Psalm 34:7) to bring safety, protection, and an abundant outpouring of blessings today for each family member and all that pertains to our lives (Hebrews 1:14). Our God shall supply all our needs according to His riches in glory by Christ Jesus (Philippians 4:19). We draw a holy Blood line in the Spirit around our families and declare that no weapon formed against us can prosper (Isaiah 54:17), and no plague shall come near our dwelling (Palm 91:10). We decree that the years the locusts have eaten shall be, and are being, restored (Joel 2:25).

We call forth a wave of abounding righteousness to cover our government, our nation and the Church. We call the *Ekklesia* (Matthew 16:19) into proper apostolic alignment and Kingdom destiny as a Kingdom-advancing, society-reforming governmental force in the earth. We decree a release of God's glory to sweep across all seven mountains of society: the Church, the family, government, business and finance, education, media and technology and arts and entertainment. Old wineskins are being broken in Church and government structures. Cold coals of revival fire and dry wells of awakening are being stirred, re-fired and re-opened. We call forth the new wine and a fresh fire of Revival and Reformation that will invade and rebuild our culture. We declare that we are a nation of awakening and redemption, and our best days are just ahead of us! We proclaim that Jesus Christ is Lord over all: His Kingdom shall come and His will be done on earth as it is in Heaven!

PROPHESYING OVER THE 7 MOUNTAINS OF INFLUENCE IN OUR CULTURE

*"And you, son of man, **prophesy to the mountains** of Israel, and say, 'O mountains of Israel, **hear the word of the LORD!***   Ezekiel 36:1

So we prophesy to these Mountains of Culture and say, "Hear the Word of the Lord!"

OVER THE MOUNTAIN OF THE CHURCH, WE PROPHESY:

A Triumphant Church shall arise out of apathy and compromise to **declare** God's undiluted Word. She will shine with the Glory of God, dispelling deep darkness from the people (Isaiah 60:1-2).

OVER THE MOUNTAIN OF GOVERNMENT, WE PROPHESY:

The wisdom and counsel of God spoken to the hearts of men will bring Kingdom alignment to our laws, legislative processes and judicial systems.

Our legislators are becoming servant leaders of integrity who will do justly, love mercy and walk humbly with God (Micah 6:8).

Patriotic citizens are awakening from their slumber and supporting leaders who stand strong for biblical truth, righteousness and justice for all — *born and unborn.*

OVER THE MOUNTAIN OF THE FAMILY AND YOUTH, WE PROPHESY:

A generation of youth is arising which shall embrace a *revolution of holiness,* a contagious *passion for Jesus and a love of the Truth.*

Fractured families are being restored to nurture children in love, teaching and modeling biblical principles.

OVER THE MOUNTAIN OF ARTS AND ENTERTAINMENT, WE PROPHESY:

A resurgence of God-honoring, family-oriented entertainment.

Over the mountain of Media, we prophesy:

A media culture rising that speaks the voice of Truth into our society.

Over the mountain of Education, we prophesy:

A fresh wind of the Holy Spirit to sweep every hindering, perverse, deceptive and anti-Christ spirit out of our schools.

Curricula which will nurture young people with biblical integrity and moral character.

Guardian angels around our schools to protect them from all predators, especially traffickers and drug dealers, making our schools and neighborhoods safe places to live and play.

Over the mountain of Business and Finance, we prophesy:

An ethical business culture based on the proven principles of free enterprise that will revitalize our economy and restore America's leadership in the global marketplace.

Over ALL, we prophesy:

A restoration of foundational biblical principles that will reorder our government, restructure our society, restore our families, transform our schools and bring REFORMATION to our nation!

A release of the GOODNESS OF GOD (that leads men to repentance) over our nation that will turn people's hearts back to HIM, so that America will once again be a blessed nation whose God is the Lord: "ONE nation, under GOD, INDIVISIBLE, with Liberty and Justice for ALL!"

And we prophesy a release of God's glory to sweep across all seven mountains of society: the Church, the family, government, business and finance, education, media and technology, and arts and entertainment. Old wineskins are being broken in Church and government structures. Cold coals of revival fire and dry wells of awakening are being stirred, re-fired, and re-opened. We call forth the new wine and a fresh fire of

Revival and Reformation that will invade and rebuild our culture. *We declare that we are a nation of awakening and redemption* and our best days are just ahead of us! We proclaim that Jesus Christ is Lord over all: His Kingdom shall come and His will be done on earth as it is in Heaven!

DECLARATION CONCERNING THE THREAT OF TERRORISM
(From Isaiah 59)

O Lord God of Hosts, God of Angel armies, who is mighty like You, O Lord? You have scattered Your enemies with Your mighty arm. Your right hand and Your holy arm have gained You the victory! LORD SABAOTH, we implore You to put on Your righteousness as a breastplate with Your garments of vengeance. Clad Yourself with holy zeal. Arise as our DELIVERER and raise Your standard against the enemy!

Mighty Jehovah, the covenant-keeping God, we bring You in remembrance of the blood of the martyrs upon this land. Remember the faith of our founding fathers and their holy covenant with You for the dedication of this land to the glory of God and the Gospel of the Lord Jesus Christ. Oh, Lord, do not forget or forsake this covenant, we pray. For IT IS WRITTEN: "The scepter of wickedness shall not rest on the land allotted to the righteous" (Psalm 125:3). For the sake of Your mighty Name, do not allow our enemies to triumph over us! Arise, and repay fury to Your adversaries and recompense to Your enemies!

In the Name of Jesus, we stand and declare, as God's Kingdom Representatives on earth, the severing of the cords of the wicked network of terrorist cells in this nation, including the dismantling and failure of all rogue jihadist plans. We declare exposure to any conspiracy by our own government seeking to undermine or usurp our freedoms and our sovereignty as a world leader. We proclaim disarray, confusion, defection and a holy fear of God into the enemy camp, foreign and domestic (Matthew 17:25). We declare the failure of any and all terror plots or conspiracies against the American people. And we rebuke the spirit of fear or any technological or cyber attacks **which would seek to impose martial law or immobilize people,** business and government. For the sake of our King and His Kingdom, we call forth the armies of heaven to engage in this battle and to encamp around and protect (Psalm 34:7) our borders, waterways, highways, railways, subways, shipyards, military installations, government buildings, the power grid and all public venues that could be a target for terror.

We declare over the entryways of our cities and our nation: "LIFT UP YOUR HEADS O YE GATES, AND BE LIFTED UP YE EVERLASTING DOORS, THAT THE KING OF GLORY MAY COME IN, the LORD STRONG AND MIGHTY, THE LORD MIGHTY IN BATTLE!" O LORD OF HOSTS (Psalm 24:7-10), the heavens are Yours and the earth also ... . Righteousness and justice are the foundation of Your throne" (Psalm 89:11 and 14), Establish the dominion of Your throne over our wayward nation, in the Mighty Name of Jesus and for His Glory!

PREEMPTIVE DECLARATION OVER THE NATION CONCERNING THE THREAT OF NATURAL DISASTERS

*The LORD has His way
In the whirlwind and in the storm,
And the clouds are the dust of His feet.
He rebukes the sea and makes it dry,
And dries up all the rivers ... .*   Nahum 1:3-5

***The voice of the Lord is over the waters;
The God of glory thunders;
The Lord is over many waters.
The voice of the Lord is powerful;
The voice of the Lord is full of majesty ... .***   Psalm 29:3-4

*He has made the earth by His power;
He has established the world by His wisdom,
And stretched out the heaven by His understanding.
When He utters His voice—
There is a multitude of waters in the heavens:
He causes the vapors to ascend from the ends of the earth;
He makes lightnings for the rain;
He brings the wind out of His treasuries ... .*   Jeremiah 51:15-16

And so, we appeal to our Mighty God Whose voice is *"powerful and full of majesty"*:

Mighty God, Creator of all that is, You whose majestic, powerful voice thunders over the waters and makes the earth shake, the rivers dry up and the heavens rain down ... . You Who have Your way in the wind, water, and the fire ... :

Have mercy upon us … and speak to the winds, the waves and the clouds across our nation. Calm the whirlwind (tornadoes) and the storms (hurricanes). Rebuke the turbulent sea where storms are brewing, and dry up the floodwaters that are ravaging our land. Open the storehouses of Heaven to rain down and quench the wildfires that are threatening our lives and homes.

Gracious Father, comfort and strengthen those who have lost so much. And may the Church rise and shine in this dark hour with acts of love and kindness.

Thank You that You are our stronghold in the day of trouble! Your mercies are new every morning, and great is Your faithfulness. You are good to all and Your tender mercies are over all Your works … . Amen! (Psalms 29:3-4 and 8, 145:8-9, 136, 135:7, 18:13; Nahum 1:3 and Lamentations 3:23).

PROCLAMATION TO SECURE BIBLICAL MARRIAGE

Whereas: IT IS WRITTEN:

- *"God created man in His own image ... male and female He created them"* (Genesis 1:27).
- *"A man shall leave his father and mother and be joined to his wife, and they shall become one flesh"* (Genesis 2:24).
- *"What God has joined together let no man put asunder"* (Matthew 19:6).
- *"If a man lies with a male as he lies with a woman, both of them have committed an abomination"* (Leviticus 20:13 and 18:22).
- *"The counsel of the LORD stands forever"* (Psalm 33:11).

Therefore, whereas:

- The family unit, built on the union of *one man and one woman*, is the biblical model for marriage.
- The union of one man and one woman in the holy covenant of marriage is the expression of the fullness of *God's image in the earth.*

We Declare, as God's Kingdom representatives on earth, that the current standing laws in every state which redefine marriage outside of the biblical model are **illegal** before the Court of Heaven. Therefore, in the Name of the Righteous Judge (2 Timothy 4:8), Jesus Christ our Lord, we declare an **overturning** of the present laws to line up with God's plumbline of righteousness. We call forth decisions by the Supreme Court of our land to uphold righteousness, justice and truth. We lift the Justices before the Lord and declare that His LIGHT of truth would flood their understanding (Ephesians 1:18), and that the FEAR of God (the beginning of wisdom) would be upon them (Proverbs 9:10).

We proclaim: **Let God's Kingdom government come and His will be established to bring the marriage laws in the United States of Christ into holy alignment.**

DECREE OVER THE SPIRITUAL STRONGHOLD OF FREEMASONRY

Gracious Lord, we repent on behalf of our city and government leaders who have participated in Masonic services, rituals, oaths and other ungodly activities which have brought condemnation and curses upon this city and our nation. Having authority with God over all that opposes Him (Luke 10:19), we declare exposed and annulled all unholy proclamations, covenants and curses made over our government buildings and lands through occult designs, symbols and cornerstones which have brought dishonor to You, our God and King.

We declare that **IT IS WRITTEN:**

- The Lord Jesus Christ is our King, our God, and our Righteous Judge (2 Timothy 4:8). He alone is our Chief Cornerstone (Ephesians 2:20) and our Sure Foundation (Isaiah 28:16). He "will make justice the measuring line and righteousness the plumbline. The hail will sweep away the refuge of lies, and waters will overflow the hiding place. Your covenant with death will be annulled, and your agreement with hell will not stand" (Isaiah 28:16-18).
- The Blood of the Lamb of God, Jesus Christ, has triumphed over and continues to prevail against (Colossians 2:15) all spiritual powers associated with this demonic stronghold to bind their influence and render their authority null and void.

We ask, Mighty God, that You would set the captives free from the deception and bondage of Freemasonry. For the sake of your Holy Name, open the eyes of those Masons who call themselves Christians. Give them a spirit of wisdom and revelation in the knowledge of God, that the eyes of their understanding will be enlightened (Colossians 1:9 and Ephesians 1:18). *Sweep away this "refuge of lies," with its false covenants, false worship and false decrees, and cleanse our city from this defilement and its influences. Quell this "fountain of sin and uncleanness" which has sprung forth from Boston (originally) and cause the (false) prophet and the unclean spirit to depart from the land* (Zechariah 13:1-2).

WE DECLARE OVER AMERICA:
- That the Lord Jesus Christ is King forever (Psalm 10:16), and HE is "the blessed and ONLY Potentate, the King of kings and Lord of lords" (2 Timothy 6:15)!
- That we shall be a nation whose God is the Lord, and that Blessed are the people whom God has chosen for His inheritance (Psalm 33:12)!
- Righteousness, Justice and Peace: a bright future, a good welfare and a fulfilled destiny (Jeremiah 29:11)!

DECREE OF HEALING AND RESTORATION OVER THE FIRST NATIONS PEOPLES

O God of mercy and forgiveness, we bring our First Nations brothers before your Throne of grace and ask that You would forgive **us** for our sins against these people. Forgive **us** for our lack of mercy, compassion and kindness. Forgive **our forefathers** for usurping their homelands and destroying their culture, and forgive **us** for abandoning them on tribal reservations today.

- O **Lord our Healer** (Exodus 15:26), remove the reproach of broken covenants and the shedding of innocent blood which have defiled this land. And heal the years of heartache and hopelessness which this has brought to innocent people.
- O **God of all Comfort** (2 Corinthians 1:3-4) and Peace (Romans 16:20), come and bring the fullness of Your *Shalom* — peace, safety, fullness, tranquility, wholeness, completeness, health, prosperity, harmony, security and well-being — to these wounded people.
- O **Lord of the Harvest** (Luke 10:2), send laborers out to bring forth a bountiful harvest from the Gospel seeds that were planted centuries ago by European missionaries who came to bring peace and redemption to this land.
- O **God of Reconciliation** (2 Corinthians 5:17-18), bring Your healing and reconciliation to restore ALL Americans to become "one nation, under God, indivisible, with liberty and justice for all."

In the name of Jesus and for His Glory and His Kingdom's sake.

PRAYER TO EXPOSE AND END HUMAN TRAFFICKING

Gracious Father, we come in the Name of Your Precious Son and our mighty Redeemer and King, Jesus Christ, Who came to set the captives free, and we ask for the souls and the lives of **all** who are caught in the evil web of human trafficking.

We ask that You would stir every heart throughout the Body of Christ into action to combat slavery in **all** of its forms. Thank You, Lord, for those who labor as modern-day abolitionists to bring an end to this nefarious scourge. Give law enforcement officers and under- cover agents supernatural revelation to uncover the hiding places and sex houses. Mobilize teams of intercessors and rescue workers to bring hope and shelter to trafficked victims.

And may the *God of Hope* fill all victims of abuse with the joy and peace in believing in Him, that they may even *abound in Hope* by the power of the Holy Spirit (Romans 15:13).

It is a shameful fact that in America, while the rest of the world is partying on Super Bowl Sunday, thousands are being sold as sex slaves at the mercy of the lusts of evil men. Father, first of all, *forgive us* for embracing a culture that would allow this to happen. And *forgive us* for desecrating *Your* day with this abominable activity. Have *mercy on us* for turning our eyes away from this problem because it may not directly touch our personal lives.

From the perpetrators to the victims, many are caught in this evil web of destruction. IT IS WRITTEN that the goodness of God leads men to repent and turn from their wicked ways. So, we call down the goodness of God over our nation on this day. May the liberating presence and goodness of Almighty God invade the strongholds of darkness to expose the hidden places of abuse and cause men to abandon their evil plans. We declare that *no money* will change hands in the abuse of women and children on Super Bowl Sunday this year. We call forth the *angelic hosts of heaven* to direct rescue teams and law enforcement officers to the location of the captives and set them free.

We stand positioned with Christ in the heavenly realms, and from that place of victory we declare a massive unraveling of the sex trafficking industry which will roll like a tsunami wave across our nation and around the world.

In the name of Jesus Christ, Who came to set the captives free. AMEN!

SHALOM AS A WEAPON OF WARFARE

The Hebrew word *shalom* is comprised of four Hebrew letters, which, when read in order, declare that shalom: DESTROYS THE AUTHORITY THAT ESTABLISHES CHAOS. Chaos exists on many levels: at the cellular level chaos brings disease; in relationships it brings contention and strife; in government it brings confusion, corruption, and the spirit of anti-Christ.

- As a part of the armor of God, we wear the Gospel of *Shalom* on our **feet: Ephesians 6:15** - "*... and having shod your **feet** with the preparation of the gospel of **peace** ...*"
- **Romans 16:20**: "*The God of **Shalom** will soon crush satan **under our feet**.*"

KINGDOM DOMINION POSITIONING:

We are seated with Christ in heavenly places and the devil is **under our feet!**

- **Ephesians 1:20-22**: "*... which He worked in Christ when He raised Him from the dead and seated Him at His right hand in the heavenly places, far above all principality and power and might and dominion, ... And He put all things **under His feet**.*"
- **Ephesians. 2:6**: "*But God, ... made **us** sit together in the heavenly places in Christ Jesus.*"

HERE IS THE PICTURE:

Satan is the authority that establishes chaos; but as we, who are seated with Christ in heavenly places, corporately walk in our Kingdom authority in the **shalom** of God, chaos is crushed and wholeness and order prevail.

BLESSING:

In the Name of Yeshua, the Prince of Shalom, I invoke the Shalom of God over you. As His Shalom fills you, all negativity, confusion and distress is dissolved. Receive His Divine order, wholeness and peace in your mind, soul and spirit.

HEALING:

And may the Shalom of God fill every cell of your body, expunging all illness and bringing the fullness of Divine health and healing.

DECLARATION:

As God's Kingdom representative on earth, as I walk on this mountain of government (and on my various Kingdom assignments), **with my feet shod with the Gospel of peace,** I declare that the atmosphere in this place will shift as the Shalom of God destroys the authority that brings chaos, confusion and contention, and His order of completeness, wholeness and clarity is ushered in.

DECLARING SHALOM OVER CITIES EXPERIENCING VIOLENCE (SHALOM DESTROYS THE AUTHORITY THAT ESTABLISHES CHAOS)

WE DECLARE THE **SHALOM** OF GOD OVER:

- Hearts fraught with fear, anger and retribution.
- Minds captivated by hatred, suspicion and wounds of the past.
- Neighborhoods and homes of innocent families.
- City streets where violent mobs are gathered.
- Crowds stirred up by embedded agitators.
- Hospitals that need to be prepared to aid the injured.
- Firefighters and rescue workers as they respond to calls.
- The police force as they work to assuage anger and quell violence.

PRAYER FOR THE UNITED STATES IN RESPONSE TO THE GETTYSBURG ADDRESS

The Gettysburg Address by President Abraham Lincoln, given on November 19, 1863:

*Four score and seven years ago our fathers brought forth on this continent, a new nation, **conceived in Liberty, and dedicated to the proposition that all men are created equal.** Now we are engaged in a great civil war, testing whether that nation, or any nation so conceived and so dedicated, can long endure. We are met on a great battlefield of that war. We have come to dedicate a portion of that field, as a final resting place for those who here **gave their lives that that nation might live.** It is altogether fitting and proper that we should do this.*

*But, in a larger sense, we cannot dedicate—we cannot consecrate—we cannot hallow—this ground. The brave men, living and dead, who struggled here, have consecrated it, far above our poor power to add or detract. The world will little note, nor long remember what we say here, but it can never forget what they did here. It is for us the living, rather, to be dedicated here to the unfinished work which they who fought here have thus far so nobly advanced. It is rather for us to be here dedicated to the great task remaining before us—**that from these honored dead we take increased devotion to that cause for which they gave the last full measure of devotion—that we here highly resolve that these dead shall not have died in vain—that this nation, under God, shall have a new birth of freedom— and that government of the people, by the people, for the people, shall not perish from the earth.***

A PRAYER AND PLEDGE

THE PRAYER: Gracious Father, as we consider the present fallen state of our homeland, even as President Lincoln did in his day, we agree and declare that this nation of the United States of America was conceived "under GOD," birthed in LIBERTY, and "dedicated to the proposition that all men are created EQUAL." And so we implore You, Father, to remember the Founders' vision: Heal our divisions, revive our righteous foundations and turn our hearts back to You, so that we may be restored as *"one nation under God, indivisible, with Liberty and Justice for all."*

THE PLEDGE: As we ponder the birth pangs of this great nation, we remember and honor the many who have given their lives, not simply that we may live, but that we may *flourish*. It is through Your Hand, O God, that we have become the greatest nation in all history — extending the banner of hope and freedom to the entire world. And so we embrace the charge of President Lincoln to take up the cause that the brave men who laid down their lives on the Gettysburg Battlefield should not have died in vain. And we pledge to do all that is in our power, through prayer and action, so *that this nation, **under God**, shall have a **new** birth of freedom — and that government **of** the people, **by** the people, and **for** the people, shall not perish from the earth.

A PROPHETIC RESPONSE TO PRESIDENT DONALD J. TRUMP'S 2017 INAUGURAL ADDRESS

In his Inaugural address, President Donald Trump made some decisive declarations that will frame the future direction of America. In his opening remarks, he said that *January 20th 2017 will be remembered as "the day of the transfer of power, when the people became the rulers of this nation again."*

Accepting this transfer of power, **we agree with and declare that we, the citizens of America, are now joined together *with* God in a great national effort to rebuild our country and to restore its promise for all of our people.**

As President Trump took his oath of office, he declared an *"oath of allegiance to all Americans. We share one heart, one home, and one glorious destiny."* Quoting from the Bible, President Trump said, *"How good and pleasant it is when God's people live together in unity."*

"When America is united, America is totally unstoppable."

IT IS WRITTEN that Unity brings down the blessings from God. **So, Father, we ask You to pour out a Spirit of Unity across our land, to bring forth the destiny that You have for America – "One nation, under God, indivisible, with liberty and justice for all."**

President Trump *"issued a new decree* **that 'from** this day **forward,** *a new vision* **will govern our land. From this moment on, it's going to be** *America First.'* **"Lord, will You bless and breathe life into President Trump's declarations:**

- **America will start winning again, winning like never before.**
- America will **seek and secure friendship and goodwill with the nations of the world.**
- America will **reinforce old alliances and form new ones and unite**

the civilized world against Radical Islamic Terrorism, which will be eradicated from the face of the earth.

President Trump's recurring theme was a *"total allegiance to the (Constitutional) vision of the United States of America" and a call to patriotism and unity:* "When you open our heart to patriotism, there is no room for prejudice. ... A new national pride will stir our souls, lift our sights, and heal our divisions."

Father, will You bless and breathe life into President Trump's call to patriotism and Unity. Together (with God's help),

- We Will Make America Strong Again.
- We Will Make America Wealthy Again.
- We Will Make America Proud Again.
- We Will Make America Safe Again.
- Our country will thrive and prosper again.
- Together, We Will Make America Great Again.

In his closing remarks, President Trump declared that this country *is protected, and will always be protected by the military and law enforcement and, most importantly, we are protected by God."*

Father, extend Your hand of mercy, grace and protection over our nation. Restore our foundation of Freedom and Liberty. And bring forth your LIFE and HEALING, so that America will once again be a light shining to the nations of the world. From a prophetic word from Johnny Enlow:

> *Heaven is in a very interventionist mode with America at this time, and it is going to take some getting used to for many who don't understand America's assigned role among the nations. **The United States was formed and fashioned with a foundation of freedom and liberty***

as a gift to the nations. *The nations of the world were hopelessly stuck in dead-end cycles of tyranny, war, and devastation. America was and still is the interruption into those cycles, and the call extends well beyond anything we have so far seen.*

Following the massacre on the Gettysburg battlefield, President Abraham Lincoln spoke these words of hope for the future of the deeply-divided nation: "... that *this nation, under God, shall have a new birth of freedom —* and that government <u>of</u> **the people,** <u>by</u> **the people,** <u>for</u> **the people, shall not perish from the earth." President Trump's Inaugural address echoes this declaration by President Lincoln.**

So, WE CALL FORTH a NEW BIRTH OF FREEDOM AND UNITY over THIS nation, that this new government OF THE PEOPLE, BY THE PEOPLE and FOR THE PEOPLE *will not perish from the earth!*

IT IS WRITTEN: **"Blessed is the nation whose God is the Lord."** So, Father, we pray that You will honor the declarations of President Trump and fulfill Your purposes concerning the national destiny for America. **For without Your intervention to bring America back to God, we are without hope.** As John Adams said, *"Our (God-breathed) Constitution* **was made only for a** *moral and religious* **people. It is wholly inadequate to the government of any other."**

CHAPTER 2

GOVERNMENTAL

GOVERNMENTAL DECREES
(TO MAKE ON SITE)

Mighty God, every place my foot treads, I am taking this land for You, for Your Kingdom, for Your Glory! I declare the Dominion of Your Throne over this Capitol Hill. I call forth Your Divine purposes and prophetic destiny over this nation that were set in place before time began. I proclaim that Your Kingdom come and Your will be done here in this city.

I stand on this **mountain of government** and call forth into this legislative body servant leaders with integrity who *do justly, love mercy, and walk humbly with their God* (Micah 6:8). As I walk with my feet shod with the Gospel of Peace, **the SHALOM of God destroys the authority that brings chaos and ushers in His Divine order** (Ephesians 6:15 and Romans 16:20).

I stand as a priest (1 Peter 2:9 and Revelation1:6) between God and our leaders, and:

- Proclaim the **Redemptive, Life-giving power of the BLOOD of CHRIST** over their lives.
- Call them into **life-changing encounters with the Living God** so that Christ may dwell in their hearts by faith (Ephesians 3:17).
- Pray that **LIGHT would flood their darkened minds** so that they would be filled with the fullness of God and the *knowledge of His will in all wisdom* and spiritual understanding (Ephesians 1:18 and 3:19).
- Pray for God to pour out His **Holy Spirit** over them **"so that it would be for His Glory to give us victory through them."** [1]

---

1. This one-sentence prayer, divinely given to Derek Prince, turned the course of WWII in the North Africa campaign, and, in effect, turned the course of the war toward an Allied victory and secured the land that was to become the nation of Israel.

Isaiah 33:22: "For the LORD IS OUR JUDGE, THE LORD IS OUR LAWGIVER, THE LORD IS OUR KING; HE WILL SAVE US."

This is the scripture the Founders used to establish our three branches of government: Judicial, Legislative and Executive.

As Watchmen we proclaim:

- The *victory of **Justice*** over lawlessness.
- The *authority of God's **Law*** across our land.
- The *majesty and Lordship of Jesus our **King*** over our Nation.

ISAIAH 22:22 DECLARATIONS OVER CITIES

Scriptures:

*The key of the house of David
I will lay on his shoulder;
So he shall open, and no one shall shut;
And he shall shut, and no one shall open.*   Isaiah 22:22

Righteousness and justice are the foundation of Your throne ... .
                                                            Psalm 89:14

God ... raised us up together, and made us sit together in the heavenly places in Christ Jesus.   Ephesians 2:6

Seated with Christ in the heavenly places, we are God's governing force on the earth. From this position of Kingdom authority, we take the Key of the House of David which we have been given to legislate into the earth realm, **such that God's throne of righteousness and justice is re-established within our land.**

So we OPEN the spiritual doors/gates of this city to:

- **The King of Glory**! (Psalm 24).
- **The Shalom of God** which destroys the authority that brings chaos.
- **Servant leaders with integrity** who do justly, love mercy and walk humbly with God (Micah 6:8).
- **The light and revelation of the Holy Spirit** that will impact the minds of our leaders and lead them into life-changing encounters with Truth (Jesus is THE Truth, John 14:6).
- **The righteous and just will of God** to prevail over the legislative process.

- **The wisdom and counsel of God** to influence the minds of the politicians and to direct all decision making.
- **Foundational biblical principles** to restructure and reestablish our government. **The River of God** to flow through the halls of government and bring forth spiritual LIFE.

AND WE CLOSE THE SPIRITUAL DOORS/GATES INTO THIS CITY TO:

- **Every perverse spirit that would exalt itself against the knowledge of God,** including the spirits of deception, falsehood, pride, rebellion, idolatry, greed, lust, lawlessness, covenant-breaking and homosexuality.
- The spirit of murder that drives the culture of death and seeks innocent blood.
- The spirits of competition, disunity and control which hinder the political process.
- Every evil and familiar spirit that would work to bring forth death and destruction.
- All compromise of the Word and Truth of God.

PRAYING FOR THE PRESIDENT:
(WISDOM, PROTECTION AND GODLY CHARACTER)

FOR WISDOM:

Father, we lift up the President and pray that You would impart to him wisdom liberally from above to make the decisions that he needs to make today (James 1:5). Each morning, awaken his ear to hear as the learned (Isaiah 50:4), and quicken his heart to be willing and wise to do the work that You have given him to do (Exodus 35:5 and 36:2). May he "be filled with the knowledge of God's will in all wisdom and spiritual understanding" (Colossians 1:9), and may the eyes of his understanding be enlightened with Your truth (Ephesians 1:18).

Your Word says that "he who rules over men must be just, ruling in the fear of God" (2 Samuel 23:3). We pray that the President would rule in the fear of God rather than men. We loose him from the influence of falsehood, deception and the influence of ungodly council and bind his mind, will and emotions to truth and the will and purposes of God. We loose him from the passions of the flesh and worldly thinking and bind him to the mind of Christ (1 Corinthians 2:16). Thank You for giving him discernment to know Your voice so that he will not follow the voice of a stranger (John 10:4-5). We pray that he would be empowered with all wisdom and knowledge so that he will be able to excel in all his accomplishments (Ephesians 3:20), to uphold righteousness, truth and justice across this land (Isaiah 28:17).

FOR PROTECTION:

Father, we declare the precious Blood of Jesus over the President, his family, and his staff. Dispatch your angels to watch over them and keep them in all their ways today (Psalm 91:11). May the Angel of the Lord encamp around the President and deliver him from every evil. May You deliver him from all his fears and save him out of all his troubles (Psalm 34:7, 4 and 6). We declare that no weapon formed against him shall prosper, and every tongue that rises up against him in judgment he shall condemn (Isaiah 54:17). We pray that You would hide him from the secret plots of the wicked, "from the rebellion of the workers of iniquity, who sharpen their tongue like a sword" (Psalm 64:2). Lord, close the mouths of those who would shoot out bitter words, and cause them to stumble over their own tongue. Keep him from the snares the enemy has laid for him and from the traps of the workers of iniquity. Let the wicked fall into their own nets, while he escapes safely (Psalm 141:9-10). Bless the President, Lord, and surround him with Your shield of favor and mercy (Psalms 5:12 and 32:10).

FOR SALVATION AND GODLY CHARACTER:

Father, we pray that the President, if he doesn't already know You, would have a life-changing encounter with You. We pray that he would have the "excellent spirit" of Daniel (Daniel 5:12), and that he would "put on the Lord Jesus Christ and make no provision for the flesh" (Romans 13:14). We loose him from fear and intimidation and bind him to power, love and a sound mind (2 Timothy1:7). We pray that discretion will protect him, and understanding will guard him, and that wisdom will save him from the ways of evil and from wicked men (Proverbs 2:10-12). I pray that he would walk worthy of the Lord, fully pleasing Him, being fruitful in every good work and increasing in the knowledge of God. Lord, may You strengthen him with might by Your glorious power, giving him patience, joyful endurance and a thankful heart (Colossians 1:10-12). **Through the Holy Spirit, may he become** a vessel for honor, sanctified and useful for the Master, prepared to **accomplish every good work for the sake of this nation, our prophetic destiny and for the Glory of Your Holy Name** (2 Timothy 2:21).

DECLARATION OVER THE JUDICIAL SYSTEM

O, Lord, You are our Judge, our Lawgiver and our King (Isaiah 33:22). You set up governments and rulers (Romans 13:1), and You founded the government of the United States as "one nation under God." In the authority and power of Jesus' name, we rebuke the adversary who has been attempting to destroy our righteous foundation through our court system and the rule of law. We declare that every plan and scheme of the devil to divert and dismantle God's model for the United States Judiciary is null and void. We call every judge in this nation to salvation and submission to the Lordship of Jesus Christ. We call every judge, from the highest court in our land to the lowest precinct, to come into alignment with the purposes and the laws of God. We call judges to fulfill their constitutional roles of upholding justice through interpreting the law and not legislating it. We call each judge to make rulings according to God's justice and Word of Truth.

We call upon You, our Righteous Judge (2 Timothy 4:8), to *abolish judicial tyranny from our land!* We declare justice the measuring line and righteousness the plumbline (Isaiah 28:17) over this nation. We call the 7-fold Spirit of God to give every judge a Spirit of wisdom, understanding, counsel, might and knowledge. May the fear of the Lord be their delight, so they will not judge by the sight of their eyes, nor the hearing of their ears, but with righteousness and equity (Isaiah 11:2-4).

O *Master of Breakthroughs* (2 Samuel 5:19), breakthrough the filibustering spirit and any other hindrances that are preventing any righteous judges from being confirmed into their God-appointed positions. In the authority of Jesus Christ, we crush, smash and destroy the spiritual strongholds that are preventing God's will and purposes from going forth through our Justice system, and that are denying or threatening the integrity of the U.S. Constitution. I rebuke, bind and cast out every spirit of witchcraft (intimidation and control), obstruction, destruction, lawlessness, division, perversion and murder. And we declare that their assignment against the Judicial System of the United States is canceled, in Jesus' name, and by the power of His shed Blood. Sovereign Lord, "the heavens are Yours, (and) the earth also … . You have a mighty arm; strong is Your hand and high is Your right hand. Righteousness and justice are the foundation of Your throne" (Psalm 89:11 and 13-14). Establish the dominion of Your throne over our courts, our lives and our wayward nation, in Jesus' name and for His glory!

DECLARATION OVER THE SUPREME COURT
(Couched it in the Revised Greek Text translation of the Lord's Prayer, represented by the italicized words)

Our Father in the heavens, the only Righteous Judge (2 Timothy 4:8),

Let Your Name be sanctified NOW, in this very moment.

Let Your Kingdom come NOW, into this present situation.

Let Your will come into being NOW, in this present moment on earth as it is already in heaven.

According to Your perfect will, we declare:

Over this Court:

That Justice is the measuring line and Righteousness is the plumbline (Isaiah 28:17), and the scepter of wickedness shall not rest on this court in this land allotted to the righteous (Psalm 125:3).

Over every Justice:

"The Spirit of wisdom, understanding, counsel, might and knowledge. May the fear of the Lord be their delight, so they will not judge by the sight of their eyes or the hearing of their ears, but with righteousness and equity" (Isaiah 11:2-4).

We implore You, Mighty God, our true Judge, Lawgiver and King, save us (Isaiah 33:22) from any decisions that would deny or threaten the integrity of the US Constitution, dishonor You, bring harm to our citizens or weaken our sovereignty as a nation.

For the sake of Your Holy Name and *because the Kingdom is Yours, and the Power and the Glory unto the end of the ages. Amen!*

DECLARING LIGHT INTO THE DARKNESS OF THE STATE DEPARTMENT

Mighty God, we worship Your Majesty as *"the blessed and only Sovereign, the King of kings and Lord of lords."* To You be honor and eternal dominion! We rejoice that You are the Light of the world (John 8:12), and that Your Light rules and reigns, unchallenged in the heavens! We declare that Your Glorious Light is obliterating the hidden works and structures of darkness erected within the State Department. Release Your **Light and Justice** to reveal the hidden places where all works of evil are being planned and perpetrated. Execute Your judgements against the forces of darkness that are manipulating men to subvert this administration. And send your heavenly Hosts to set these captives free to run to the **LIGHT!**

LIGHT of the world, we agree for the victory of Your Light. May **the very foundations of evil be usurped by Your Illuminating Presence this day!** May the State Department become a *House of Light* on Capitol Hill, and may the nations represented therein carry Your Light into all the world.

PROCLAMATION OVER NATIONAL SECURITY

O Most Merciful Father, I lift up America and ask You to hold her in Your secret place (Psalm 91:1) under the shadow of Your wings (Psalm 17:8). As you raised Your mighty voice to call the world into being (Psalm 33:6), may You raise Your mighty voice to roar (Joel 3:16) against the spirit of death and the tactics of terror and destruction. May You "frustrate the devices of the crafty so that their hands cannot carry out their plans" (Job 5:12). Lord, Your mercies endure forever! Thank You for protecting this nation from natural disasters as well as terrorist, biochemical and nuclear attacks.

I proclaim the Blood of Jesus over our defense and telecommunication systems, particularly satellite, computer, Internet, telephone and all other media networks, and also over our energy systems and nuclear power plants. I thank You that Your angelic host encamps around and protects (Psalm 34:7) our high risk and strategic locations: subway and rail systems, airports and airplanes, oil refineries and storage areas, bridges, reservoirs, seaports, waterways, dams, shipyards and military bases. I declare the efficacy of the "bio-watch" systems around our cities and the heightened security systems around our airports.

I proclaim that America will fulfill her God-ordained destiny to be a Light shining to the nations, and to take the Gospel to all the earth! May Your Kingdom come and Your will be done in, for and through America

In Jesus' name and for His Glory!

CHAPTER 3

THE CHURCH

PRAYER FOR THE CHURCH REGARDING ISRAEL
(One New Man)

Father, I call forth spiritual leaders within the Church that would have a true burden and love for Israel, Your chosen people, and the "apple of Your eye" (Zechariah 2:8). I repent for the anti-Semitic spirit which has pervaded the Church and for the false belief that the Church has replaced Israel in God's prophetic and redemptive plan. Forgive us, Father, and give us hearts that love Israel as You do. Give Your Church revelation from Your Word that You are shaping history for two groups of covenanted people, Israel and the Church, whom You are bringing together as ONE NEW MAN (Ephesians 2:11-16). I call the Church to understand that both her heritage and her destiny lie with the Jewish people. May the Jews and the Gentile Christians be built together into a glorious holy temple fit for Your dwelling place in the earth (Ephesians 2:21-22)!

SCRIPTURAL DECLARATIONS FOR PASTORS

I PROCLAIM THAT BY THE ENABLING GRACE OF GOD:

- They would be built up in their most holy faith ... (Jude 20), so that they would persevere as Nehemiah did rebuilding the wall of Jerusalem (Nehemiah).
- They would endure chastening, knowing that God deals with them as sons (Hebrews 12:9).
- They would stand on the truth that nothing can separate them from God's love, and that they are more than conquerors through Jesus (Romans 8:35-37).
- They would hold fast the confidence and rejoicing of hope firm to the end (Hebrews 3:6).
- As they have received Christ, so shall they walk in Him, rooted and built up in Him and established in the faith, as they have been taught, abounding in it, with thanksgiving (Colossians 2:6).
- They would be strong, immovable, always abounding in the work of the Lord, knowing their labor is not in vain (1 Corinthians 15:58).
- They would fully submit to God and victoriously resist the devil; remaining steadfast, knowing Jesus and His brothers have experienced the same sufferings (James 4:7 and 1 Peter 5:9).
- They would stand fast in liberty, not being entangled again with bondage (Galatians 5:1).
- They would press on toward the goal of the prize of the upward call of Christ, laying aside every weight and besetting sin, and running the race with endurance to receive the crown (Philippians 3:14 and Hebrews 12:1-2).
- Freedom of utterance would be given them that they would open their mouths boldly, to make known the mystery of the gospel, and that signs and wonders would follow the preaching of the Word (Ephesians 6:19 and Acts 4:29-30).

- They would have great boldness of faith which is in Christ Jesus (1 Timothy 3:13).
- They would be clothed with humility, which brings grace; and the fear of the Lord, which brings wisdom (1 Peter 5:5, and Proverbs 22:4 and 1:7).
- They might be strengthened, perfected and established in the power of God's might and by the glory of God's grace (1 Peter 5:10 and Ephesians 6:10).
- They would fear God more than men, and preach the **complete and undiluted** Gospel in their churches.
- They would care more about building the **Kingdom of God** than advancing their own ministries.

A PROPHETIC CALL FOR THE RISE OF THE EKKLESIA IN UNITY AND HOLY ALIGNMENT

Forgive us, Lord, for dissension, division and competition within the Body of Christ. Pour out Your Glory upon us, to bring us into a Spirit of unity, so that we might become one as You and the Father are one, as a witness to the world of Your great love (John 17:20-23).

I call the Church into Your Divine order under the Apostolic Headship. I call each member of the Body to take his own place in the assembly, being "fitly joined together" (Ephesians 4:16, KJV), so as please You, and not us (1 Corinthians 12:18). I call forth the activation of the functional ministry of apostles, prophets, evangelists, pastors and teachers into each individual church and into the corporate Body, for our equipping and edification, for the unity of the faith, and for the perfecting of Your character within us (Ephesians 4:11-16).

Mighty God, arise in Your zeal to stir up and activate the gifts that You have deposited within the Church: words of wisdom and knowledge, faith, gifts of healings, working of miracles, discerning of spirits, prophecy, tongues and interpretation, helps and administrations (1 Corinthians 12:7-10 and 28). Holy Father, forgive us for being an impotent spiritual force in the world, "bringing forth wind," and not accomplishing any deliverance in the earth (Isaiah 26:18). *It is time for the Ekklesia to arise! I call forth Your mighty army, well equipped for battle and for labor in Your harvest fields,*

In Jesus' name and for His glory!
(Ephesians 6:10-11 and Luke 10:2)

PUTTING ON THE "NEW MAN"

I call the Church to purify yourselves from "everything that contaminates body and spirit, perfecting holiness out of reverence for God" (2 Corinthians 7:1).

Father, bring a deep conviction and repentance upon Your Body so that we would have eyes to see our nakedness and be willing to pay the price that You require for purity. Send Your refining fire to purge us and bring forth pure gold: the beauty of holiness (Psalm 96:9) within (Revelation 3:16-18). Help us to put on the character of Your "chosen people ... clothing ourselves with compassion, kindness, humility, gentleness, patience, forgiveness, love, unity, peace and thankfulness" (Colossians 3:12-17). Help us "put off our former conduct and the old man which grows corrupt according to the deceitful lusts, and be renewed in the spirit of (our) mind(s)," putting on the "new man which was created according to God, in true righteousness and holiness" (Ephesians 4:22-24). The hour has come to awake out of our slumber! *I call the NEW MAN to arise!*

Church, awake and put aside the deeds of darkness and put on the armor of light! Renounce orgies and drunkenness, sexual immorality and debauchery, dissension and jealousy and clothe yourself with the Lord Jesus Christ, not considering how to gratify the desires of the sinful nature" (Romans 13:11-14, NIV)!

PRAYER FOR REPENTANCE AND PURITY

PURIFYING THE BRIDE

Lord Jesus, heal us of our carnal, aberrant Christianity. Cause us to rise up in authentic Christianity that glorifies You in the world. May Your pure, spotless Bride come forth in all her splendor (Ephesians 5:27). May the Church arise out of fear and doubt into overcoming faith, to sit with You on Your throne (Revelation 3:21). Father, purge the Church of our complacency, compromise and apathy (Malachi 3:3). May we turn back to You in true repentance, with a holy fear of God, a holy hatred of sin and a holy passion for Jesus in our hearts.

Forgive us, Lord, for filling the soccer fields, football stadiums and amusement parks on Sunday mornings instead of filling Your churches. I call the Church to rise up out of lukewarmness, to be "white-hot enthusiastic lovers of our God," clothed with true humility instead of being driven by pride. May the Church humble herself in Your sight and give up her prideful ways (James 4:10) and childish things, and be perfected in Your holiness and love (1 Corinthians 13:10-11). Forgive us, Father, for our friendship with the world that has made us Your enemies (James 4:4). Help us, instead, to hunger and thirst after righteousness (Matthew 5:6).

Lord, increase our appetite for the things that attract Your Presence — love and compassion for our neighbors (Matthew 22:39), love and devotion to You (Matthew 22:37), repentant and contrite hearts (Psalm 51:17), obedience (John 14:15), holiness (1 Peter 1:15-16), unity (Ephesians 4:3), faith (Hebrews 11:6), effective and fervent praying (James 5:16), and true spiritual worship that will tear down idols and strongholds (John 4:23). And send Your holy refining fire to purge from us all of those things that repel Your Presence — complacency, compromise, apathy (Ephesians 5:11), bitterness (Hebrews 12:15), anger (Ephesians 4:31), unforgiveness (Mark 11:25), offense (Romans 14:13), envy (Romans 1:29), impurity (Hebrews 12:14), pride (1 John 2:16), lukewarmness (Revelation 3:16) — and every other work of the flesh that stifles spiritual life and are withholding Your blessing and manifest Presence from us. Lord, may we be the salt and light in the world that You have called us to be (Matthew 5:13-14)! Expand our vision! Revive the eternity that you have put in our hearts (Ecclesiastes 3:11)!

Church, it is time to "awake, awake you who sleep, come arise from the dead and Christ will give you light! You are the LIGHT of the world! So arise and shine, for your light has come and the Glory of the Lord is risen upon you (Ephesians 5:14, Matthew 5:15 and Isaiah 60:12)!

CHAPTER 4
ISRAEL

PRAYING FOR THE PEACE OF JERUSALEM
(from Psalm 122)

O Jerusalem, may peace and prosperity be within your walls. For the sake of God's chosen ones, I say, 'Peace be within you.' Come, Prince of Peace (Isaiah 9:6); establish peace for Israel (Isaiah 26:12) and make Jerusalem a strong city. Appoint salvation for walls and open the gates that Israel may once again be that righteous and peaceful nation which keeps the truth and "whose mind is stayed on You" (Isaiah 26:1-3).

Lord, may You command your blessing over Israel. May Your oil of peace and unity be poured out on that land like oil was upon the beard of Aaron, refreshing as the dew of Herman, descending upon the mountains of Zion (Psalm 133). May the Jewish and Arab descendants of Abraham live together in peace, love and justice on your hallowed soil. Father, bring Revival to the land of Israel and turn the hearts of the Jews and Arabs toward Messiah, the God of Israel, His Word and His purposes!

O Jerusalem, because of the house of the Lord our God, I seek your good. I pray for the peace of Jerusalem; and may all who love you prosper.

PRAYING FOR A REVELATION
OF MESSIAH

O Holy One of Israel (Psalm 89:18), I bring You in remembrance that Your covenant with Israel through David was an everlasting covenant (1 Chronicles 17:11-14). I pray that the devil's strategies to bring terror and destruction to Israel will backfire and that You will turn the evil perpetrated against Your Chosen Ones to good (Genesis 50:20).

Father, I pray that You will orchestrate the desperate heartcry that will cause the veil over their hearts (2 Corinthians 3:16) to be rent in two, and bring them into the presence of their Messiah Yeshua. O Lord, "open their understanding that they might comprehend the Scriptures" (Luke 24:45), so that "in their affliction they will earnestly seek (God) … and acknowledge their offense" before Him (Hosea 5:15).

And so all Israel will be saved; as it is written, the Deliverer will come out of Zion, and He will turn away ungodliness from Jacob; for this is My covenant with them, when I take away their sins.

Romans 11:26

PROCLAMATION CONCERNING THE EXALTATION OF HOMOSEXUALITY ASSOCIATED WITH "GAY PRIDE" CELEBRATIONS IN ISRAEL

In the Name of Jesus Christ of Nazareth, we demolish the stronghold of sodomy operating out of Tel Aviv and Jerusalem and declare that the Blood of Jesus has triumphed over you (Colossians 2:15). We take authority over and forbid (Matthew 18:18) any demonic entities which would seek to sow strife and violence at any demonstrations throughout Israel. We take the keys to the house of David (according to Isaiah 22:22) and close the door to this celebration of perversion and demonic bondage of "Gay Pride," and we open the door to freedom and wholeness of life in Messiah Yeshua.

We say to you, Tel Aviv, you are NOT the "gay capital of the world." We declare that out of your holy, blood-washed, covenant ground flows springs of living water, making you the "Deliverance and Salvation Capital" of the world (Isaiah 12:3).

O Mighty One of Israel, we call upon You to deliver Your deceived people and Your innocent children from the power of darkness and to convey them into the Kingdom of the Son of Your Love (Colossians 1:13). Father, forgive all those governmental leaders who are promoting and participating in that which is abominable to You. We demolish every argument and every pretension that sets itself up against the knowledge of God and take captive every thought to make it obedient to Christ (2 Corinthians 10:5). Father, we thank You for setting the captives free and bringing every man, woman, and child into Your Kingdom. "For thus says the LORD:

> *Even the captives of the mighty shall be taken away,*
> *And the prey of the terrible be delivered;*
> *For I will contend with him who contends with you,*
> *And I will save your children."*
>   Isaiah 49:25

PURIM DECREE OVER ISRAEL "FOR SUCH A TIME AS THIS."

We read in Esther 8:8 the words of King Xerxes:

You, yourselves, write a decree concerning the Jews, as you please, in the king's name and seal it with the king's signet ring. For whatever is written in the king's name and sealed with the king's signet ring no one can revoke.

Let us stand and intercede (as Esther did) against the decree of destruction made against Israel by the Hamans of *our* day. And let us declare a decree in the Name of Yeshua, the King of kings, and seal it with our King's signet ring — the BLOOD OF THE LAMB!

In the Name that is above every other name, Yeshua, the Christ, the King of kings and Lord of lords, we declare that the Jewish people are God's Chosen Ones and the "apple of His eye." We further declare that they hold a biblical covenant to the physical land of Israel, as IT IS WRITTEN in Genesis 17:7-8:

And I will establish My covenant between Me and you and your descendants after you in their generations, for an everlasting covenant .... Also **I will give to you and your descendants after you ... all the land of Canaan, as an everlasting possession;** *and I will be their God.*

Therefore we declare, in the Name and authority of Yeshua, Jesus Christ of Nazareth, who came in the flesh (1 John 4:3), that the Blood of Yeshua has triumphed over and continues to prevail against (Colossians 2:15) the entrenchment of all demonic forces that are empowering the evil anti-Israel confederation within the Middle East. And we ask You, Mighty God, to send forth the archangel Michael and the Hosts of Heaven to enforce this decree over Israel and to defeat the wicked kings over Persia (Middle East), according to the Word of the Lord in Daniel 10:13. We decree that the wicked spirit of Haman, who still seeks to destroy Israel, was and is defeated, according to the Word of God in Esther 8:7. We beseech You, Yeshua, the Righteous Judge (2 Timothy 4:8), to bring Your holy judgments against these wicked powers once and for all. We decree that all of these principalities and spiritual powers of darkness must bow to the Name, authority and power of Yeshua, the Christ, the King of kings and Lord of Hosts (Philippians 2:10). Jehovah Sabaoth, pursue them with Your tempest, and frighten them with Your storm. Fill their faces with shame, that they may seek Your name, O Lord ... . That they may know that You, whose name alone is the LORD, are the Most High over all the earth (Psalm 83:15-16 and18).

We proclaim this declaration sealed by the Blood of the Lamb of God, the King of kings, Yeshua, the Christ, the MIGHTY ONE of Israel!

Lord, we give You no rest until You make Jerusalem a praise in all the earth (Isaiah 62:7)!

The kingdoms of this world (shall) become the kingdoms of our Lord and of His Christ, and He shall reign forever.   Revelation 11:15

DECREES CONCERNING UNHOLY DOCTRINES OF MEN SEEKING TO DIVIDE UP ISRAEL'S COVENANT LAND

We decree by the power and name of Jesus Christ of Nazareth, Who came in the flesh, that any plan to give away or divide up Israel's covenant land is null and void and superseded by the Blood Covenant Israel has with Almighty God through His servant Abraham. As IT IS WRITTEN in Genesis 17:7-8:

> *And I will establish My covenant between Me and you and your descendants after you in their generations, for an everlasting covenant .... Also* **I will give to you and your descendants after you ... all the land of Canaan, as an everlasting possession;** *and I will be their God.*

So we decree: **The land is Israel's and forever shall be. Therefore, we decree that no plan, scheme or weapon formulated to divide the biblical land of Israel, the "Apple of God's Eye," shall prosper.**

We further stand in agreement with the Word of God which states that the wicked shall "take counsel together, and it shall come to naught; they shall speak the word, and it shall not stand" (Isaiah 8:10). Then, from our Kingdom positioning with Christ over all that opposes Him, we stand against the wiles of the devil and spiritual hosts of wickedness in heavenly places (Ephesians 6:11-12). We take the keys to the House of David (according to Isaiah 22:22) and close every door of access used by any *spiritual* powers sent to divide and conquer Israel, sealing these spiritual gates with the Blood of the Lamb of God, Who has defeated every foe and put to disgrace every demonic power (1 John 3:8 and Colossians 2:15).

DECREE CONCERNING THE ESTABLISHMENT OF ISRAEL IN HER COVENANT LAND

In the authority of Jesus Christ and in the power of His Name, we decree that Israel is the Lord's and all those who dwell therein (Psalm 24:1). Furthermore, IT IS WRITTEN that God's Chosen People, Israel, hold a covenant deed to all the land of Canaan (Genesis 17:7-8). So we take the keys to the House of David (Isaiah 22:22) over the City of David and open it to the KING OF GLORY, declaring: "Be lifted up you city gates of Jerusalem! And be lifted up you ancient doors in Israel, so that the KING OF GLORY may come in! The LORD OF HOSTS, THE LORD STRONG AND MIGHTY, THE LORD MIGHTY IN BATTLE (Psalm 24:7-10)!

We declare that the ancient foundations of Righteousness, Justice and Truth, along with Israel's biblical boundaries, shall be re-established as decreed in covenant with Almighty God through Abraham, Isaac and Jacob!

CHAPTER 5

THE NATIONS

DECLARING SHALOM AND KINGDOM GOVERNMENT OVER THE MIDDLE EAST

We lift up the Name of the Sovereign Lord, *Yeshua*, the Christ, over the land of the Middle East. And we ask You, Mighty God, for Your sovereign protection over the Christians in the path of destruction. We declare a halt to the murderous rampage of ISIS, and we speak the SHALOM of God into the midst of the chaos. In the Name of Jesus, we bind up and cancel the influence of every faction seeking to sow division, terror, murder and violence, and we call forth justice for all who are oppressed. We take the Keys to the House of David (Isaiah 22:22), and we close the door in the Spirit realm to the radical Islamic insurgence incited by ISIS, Al Qaeda, Hamas, Boko Haram and other Muslim terrorist groups.

In the name and power of the Lord Jesus Christ of Nazareth, who came in the flesh (1 John 4:3), we decree that the Blood of Jesus has triumphed over and prevails against the entrenchment of all demonic forces seeking dominion in the Middle East. We loose the people from the spirit of "jihad" that seeks to incite hatred, murder and revenge. We decree that the spiritual kingdom of Babylon and the stronghold of Islam must bow to the **Name, Kingdom**, and **Authority** of the **Lord Jesus Christ**. FOR IT IS WRITTEN:

- **The Name**: "God has highly exalted (Jesus) and given Him the **name** which is above every name, that at the name of Jesus every knee should bow ... and every tongue should confess that Jesus Christ is Lord ..." (Philippians 2:10-11).
- **The Kingdom**: "The kingdoms of this world (shall) become the **kingdoms** of our Lord and of His Christ, and He shall reign forever" (Revelation 11:15).
- **The Authority**: "... and the **government** will be upon His shoulder" (Isaiah 9:6). For "the LORD is our Judge, the LORD is our Lawgiver, the LORD is our King" (Isaiah 33:22).

Then, having authority with Almighty God over all that opposes Him (Luke 10:19), we take the keys to the house of David (according to Isaiah 22:22) and close the spiritual door of access used by these powers of darkness, and we declare annulled all unholy alignments and covenants against the land and people. We call the people out of the reign of darkness and death and into the Kingdom of light and truth, out of the bondage of Islam and into the Liberty of Jesus Christ. We call the lost sheep into the fold, declaring, "Their Redeemer is strong. The Lord of Hosts is His name. He will thoroughly plead their case; that He may give rest to the land and disquiet the inhabitants of Babylon" (Jeremiah 50:34).

We call forth *wells of Revival* throughout the land of the Middle East, saying, "Spring up, O well, and flood the land with the glory of God! So that with joy the people may draw water from the wells of salvation" (Numbers 21:17 and Isaiah 12:3)!

O Mighty One of Israel, we ask You to send Your warring angels to encamp around Israel (Psalm 34:7) and to seal her borders and airspace with a hedge of protection against Iran and all other enemies who would seek to destroy her. In the Name of Yeshua, Who came in the flesh, we declare that satan is bound from mobilizing the forces of evil in the Arab states surrounding Israel. We decree failure to any unholy coalition efforts to form a confederacy against You and take the pastures of God for a possession. O my God, fill their faces with shame, that they may seek Your Name, that they may know that You, whose Name alone is the LORD, are the Most High over all the earth (Psalm 83:5, 12, 16 and18).

And, finally, We decree the Word of the Lord from Psalm 24 over the Middle East, saying: "The land of the Middle East is the Lord's, and all those who dwell therein." We declare over these nations: "Be lifted up you city gates and ancient doors throughout the Middle East, so the KING OF GLORY may come in, the LORD OF HOSTS, the LORD STRONG AND MIGHTY, the LORD MIGHTY IN BATTLE." We declare that the dominion of Allah and the forces of evil aligned under that stronghold are uprooted and cast out of the Middle East, and the dominion of the Lord Jesus Christ is established! AMEN!

We ask You, LORD OF HOSTS, to call forth Your warrior angels of the heavenly host to enforce this decree (Hebrews 1:14) and to withstand this battle in the heavenlies (Daniel 10:13)!

DECREE TO COUNTER FALSE WORSHIP DURING RAMADAN AND TO SET THE CAPTIVES FREE!

There is much demonic activity that is energized out of the Muslim prayers and fasting of the season of Ramadan. We need to lift up our own fastings and prayers and raise our sword (the Word of God) against this activity and the deception of Islam and for the release of the Muslim people.

KEYS TO PRAYING FOR MUSLIMS:
1. They don't believe that God binds Himself to His people through covenants.
2. They believe that works and legalized prayer is the only way to please their god.
3. They have no guarantee of eternal reward or life in heaven, especially women.
4. They have no concept of grace, nor is love present in the Quran.
5. Their religion is based on intimidation and fear. This spirit of terror holds even whole nations and governments hostage, where Islamic leaders fear the violent reprisals of radical fundamentalists.

DECREE USING THE KEYS ABOVE:
The sword of the Spirit declares over the stronghold of deception of Islam, "Your covenant with death is annulled and your agreement with hell shall not stand" (Isaiah 28:18). For the Lord Jesus Christ has already disarmed your powers and authorities, by making a public spectacle of them, triumphing over them by the blood of His cross (Colossians 2:15). And we declare that the Blood of the Lamb of God, Jesus Christ, continues to prevail against these demonic powers. Therefore, we declare annulled the efficacy of all Islamic prayer and false worship offered to this false god.

Jesus died so that all men would be saved and set free to know and worship HIM. Therefore, we loose the Muslim people from spirits of superstition, fear and intimidation. We loose them from the Deceiver and the anti-Christ spirit — the spirit of Islam. And we bind them to the Spirit of Truth (John 14:6 and 17) and to reconciliation with God (2 Corinthians 5:20).

We praise You, Lord, that the garment of Islam, the veil that is spread over all nations (Isaiah 25:7), is being unraveled, so that those who are walking in darkness would see the Great Light of Messiah Yeshua (Isaiah 9:2 and 6)! O Lord, give them "a spirit of wisdom and revelation in the knowledge of God" (Colossians 1:9). Enlighten the eyes of their understanding (Ephesians 1:18) to see the true God, the Mighty One of Israel, Whose name alone is the Lord, the Most High over all the earth (Psalm 83:18)!

Thank You, Mighty Deliverer, for setting these captives free from a religion that imprisons them through deception, oppression and fear. Reveal Yourself to the Muslim people as the personal, covenant-keeping God Who manifests Himself to His people in grace and love. Visit them in dreams and visions of the night, when You open the ears of men and seal their instruction ... . That they might turn from their deeds, and that their souls might be rescued from the pit and their lives from perishing by the sword (Job 33:15-18)! Most High God, glorify Yourself and set the captives free during this season of Ramadan!

PRAYER FOR REVELATION FOR THE ARAB/MUSLIM PEOPLES

O Great Jehovah (the personal, covenant-keeping God Who manifests Himself to His people in grace and love), for Your name's sake, vindicate and glorify Your holy name before the heathen (Psalm 74:22)! Father, Your Word says that You "will destroy on this mountain the face of the covering cast over all people, and the veil that is spread over all nations" (Isaiah 25:7). Most merciful Father, we beseech You to cause that veil over the Arab/Muslim peoples to be rent in two so that those who are walking in darkness would see a great light, the Light of Messiah Jesus (Isaiah 9:2 and 6)!

We pray that they would no longer walk in "the futility of their mind, having their understanding darkened, (and) being alienated from the life of God, because of the ignorance that is in them, and because of the blindness of their heart" (Ephesians 4:18). Lord, give them "a spirit of wisdom and revelation in the knowledge of God" (Colossians 1:9), "that the eyes of their understanding may be enlightened" (Ephesians 1:18) to see the true God, the Mighty One of Israel, Whose name alone is the Lord, the Most High over all the earth (Psalm 83:18).

We loose their minds from the bondage of law and "works." We loose them from spirits of fear and intimidation. We loose them from the deceiver and the anti-Christ spirit (2 John 7), the spirit of Islam. And we bind them to the Spirit of Truth (John 14:6 and 17) and to reconciliation with God (2 Corinthians 5:20). We pray that all of Abraham's children would live in peace and realize their destiny in God:

Oh, that the salvation of Ishmael would come out of Islam!
When the Lord brings back the captivity of His people,
Let Ishmael rejoice and Israel be glad together!

Psalm 14:7, paraphrased

TAKING AUTHORITY AGAINST TERRORISM

AGAINST THE SPIRITUAL FORCES INCITING TERRORISM:

Arise, O Lord, in Your anger; rise up against the rage of (our) enemies (principalities, powers, rulers of darkness; spiritual wickedness in high places (Ephesians 6:12). Awake, my God, decree justice. O righteous God ... , bring an end to the violence of the wicked and make the righteous secure (Isaiah 51:9 and Psalm 7:6 and 9). For, Lord, the wicked gather themselves together against the souls of the righteous and condemn the innocent blood. Mighty God ... , cut them off in their own wickedness (Psalm 94:21). O Lord, give us help from trouble; the help of man is useless. Through God we shall do valiantly, it is He Who shall tread down our enemies (Psalm 60:11-12)!

CONCERNING THE NETWORK OF TERRORIST CELLS IN AMERICA:

Lord, You alone are righteous and cut asunder the cords of the wicked (Psalm 129:4). Lord Sabaoth, we cry out, "Cut asunder the cords of the wicked network of terrorist cells in America, and bring disarray, confusion, defection and a holy fear of God into the enemy camp." Sever their communication network, their financial funding and their tracking systems. Diffuse their power and expose their evil schemes and terrorist activities and bring them to justice, in Jesus' name.

OVER WORLD-WIDE TERRORISM:

In the authority of Jesus Christ of Nazareth and by the power of His name, we decree destruction over the world-wide terrorist network. We declare, "Let God arise over terrorism and His enemies be scattered" (Psalm 68:1)! We decree that every terrorist-sponsoring-and-supporting government shall be dismantled and uprooted. Lord of Hosts, we implore You to cause ambushments to come from within the terrorist network, so that it will begin to self-destruct from the inside out (2 Chronicles 20:22-24). We declare that the infrastructure of terrorism shall collapse in on itself as the ambushments are set by Your mighty hand and the leadership is divided and destroyed. For IT IS WRITTEN: "Every house divided against itself will not stand" (Matthew 12:25).

Over Terrorists:

Father, have mercy on the terrorists. Forgive them for they know not what they do. We cry out for the souls lost in the deception and allure of jihad. May those who would willingly sacrifice their lives to Allah receive the sacrifice of Your dear Son for them. Put the holy fear of God in their hearts. And give them eyes to see You as the Lord, Jehovah, the personal, covenant-keeping God of love. Bring them up out the pit of miry clay that has them trapped, and set their feet upon the Rock (Psalm 40:2). Deliver them from demonic power and from their prisons of hatred and destruction. O Mighty Deliverer, set the captives free (Luke 4:18), and send laborers into their harvest fields (Matthew 9:38).

Father, we pray that You would target every terrorist leader, and that, like Saul of Tarsus, You would knock them off their "high horses" of pride, delusion and deception. May the brilliance of Your Glory surround them and bring them to their knees in surrender to You (Acts 9:1-6)! We push back the occult cover of darkness that conceals them. For IT IS WRITTEN: "Their webs of evil will not become garments; nor will they cover themselves with their works." We declare, in Jesus' name, that their works will be exposed, and the perpetrators apprehended, for theirs are "works of iniquity, and the act of violence is in their hands" (Isaiah 59:6). Merciful God, You desire that all men would be saved and come to the knowledge of the truth (1 Timothy 2:4). Therefore, *may every terrorist camp become a harvest field.*

In Jesus' Name!

DECLARING LIGHT INTO THE DARKNESS OVER TERRORISM

We are seated with Christ in heavenly places *far above all principalities and powers of darkness,* and from this elevated place we worship His Majesty, the Lord and Creator of the universe and all that it holds!

> *He [Christ] is the image of the invisible God, the firstborn over all creation. For by Him all things were created that are in heaven and that are on earth, visible and invisible, whether thrones or dominions or principalities or powers. All things were created through Him and for Him. And He is before all things, and in Him all things consist. And He is the head of the body, the church, who is the beginning, the firstborn from the dead, that in all things He may have the preeminence.*
> Colossians 1:15-18

Mighty God, we worship Your Majesty as *"the blessed and only Sovereign, the King of kings and Lord of lords who rules and reigns over all . . . ."* To You be honor and eternal dominion! We rejoice that You are the Light of the world, and that **Your LIGHT rules and reigns, unchallenged in the heavens!** We declare that Your Glorious LIGHT is obliterating the hidden works of darkness generated through *false worship* in every mosque across this land! Release Your LIGHT and justice, and reveal the hiding places where abominations, cruelty and wickedness are being planned and perpetrated. Let Your LIGHT turn the hearts of those following wicked orders, that they would even turn back and expose those who are giving the orders. Let the devices, schemes, and resources for wickedness and *the forces of evil that manipulate men and keep them in bondage* be exposed by Your magnificent LIGHT! Send your Heavenly Host to set the captives free to run *to the* **LIGHT***!*

LIGHT of the world, we agree for the victory of Your Light. May the very foundations of evil be usurped by Your Illuminating Presence this day!

MOUNTING A DEFENSE AGAINST ENEMY ATTACK

In this situation, an evangelistic and rescue ministry in Africa that was saving thousands of souls and children came under attack. The enemy mounted his offense using government officials, ISIS soldiers and even people within the organization. Our response was to rise up in Kingdom authority:

In the Name of Jesus Christ, the Only Righteous Judge, we bring this situation before the Court of Heaven where the Ancient of Days presides (Daniel 7:9). And we ask, You, the Father of all Mercy, Justice and Grace, that justice be done on behalf of Your servants who stand together in this ministry. We ask you, Father, because of the precious Blood of Christ, and for the sake of Your Harvest, that You would declare Your verdict to over-rule what satan has planned against this ministry, and issue a restraining order against every demonic agenda erected to thwart justice and to steal the Harvest.

Further, we proclaim, in the Name that is above all names, Jesus the Christ, that the BLOOD of Jesus has triumphed over and continues to pre-vail against these evil agendas and every demon associated with promoting them. We declare that all demonic strategies and agendas are being thwarted, people are coming to repentance, corruption of government officials is being exposed and the victory of the Lord is established. Let GOD arise and His enemies be scattered!

We make these decrees so that many multitudes may be won for Your Kingdom through the preaching of these, young anointed street evangelists, in partnership with Your Holy Spirit. We call forth an earthshaking tidal wave of signs, wonders and miracles to sweep across Africa into every dark stronghold — in hearts and in physical enemy camps — to set the captive free, bring in the Harvest and release a whole new generation of evangelists.

And He said to them, "Go into all the world and **preach the gospel** *to every creature ... . And* **these signs will follow those who believe: In My name they will cast out demons; they will speak with new tongues; they will take up serpents; and if they drink anything deadly, it will by no means hurt them; they will lay hands on the sick, and they will recover. ... And they went out and preached everywhere, the Lord working with them** *and confirming the word through the accompanying signs.*   Mark 16:15-20

A PROPHETIC CALL TO BRING IN THE HARVEST

O **Lord of the Harvest**, send out Your laborers into Your harvest fields (Luke 10:3). Give Your people vision to see the fields that are ripe. Propel us out of our lives of complacency and apathy and into "the streets and lanes of the city, (to) bring in the poor and the maimed and the lame and the blind" (Luke 14:21). Take us out of our comfort zones and burden us with Your heart for the lost. Anoint us to go into "the highways and hedges and compel them to come in, that [Your] house may be filled" (Luke 14:23).

O **Lord of the Increase** (1 Corinthians 3:7), may the seeds You have scattered over the earth bring forth a hundred-fold Harvest for Your kingdom (Matthew 13:8)! Bring forth a spirit of repentance so that Your former and latter rain of righteousness will come and soften the soil of our hearts, so that we might break up the fallow ground and seek the knowledge of the Lord and His mercy (Hosea 6:1-3 and 10:12)!

A PROPHETIC CALL FOR PEACE

O **God of Peace**, come and crush Satan under our feet (Romans 16:20)! Bring down the evil structures of this world that hold your Harvest captive. Scatter the peoples who delight in war (Psalm 68:30). Banish the reproach of our sin so that righteousness may exalt the nations (Proverbs 14:34). May judgment return to righteousness and all the upright in heart follow it (Psalm 94:15). And may righteousness and salvation go forth in the earth as a blazing torch (Isaiah 62:1).

O God, open the blinded eyes to see the Lord and walk in His light (Isaiah 2:5). O Righteous Judge, may You hasten the day when people will "beat their swords into plowshares and their spears into pruning hooks, (so that) nation shall not lift up sword against nation, neither shall they learn war anymore" (Isaiah 2:4). Prince of Peace (Isaiah 9:6), come and establish Your throne upon this earth that Your Kingdom will come and Your will be done as it is in heaven (Matthew 6:10)!

CHAPTER 6

REVIVAL

PRAYER OF CONFESSION
AND CRY FOR REVIVAL
"AMERICA, ARISE TO YOUR DESTINY!"

Most Holy God, we confess that we have been a stiff-necked and rebellious people who have run after other gods. We have lusted after pleasures, money, fame and power. Sexual irresponsibility and perversion have polluted our nation, and the blood of the innocents cries out to You. Our sins have destroyed lives, dishonored You and defiled our land. Lord, we stand before You "wretched, miserable, poor, blind, and naked" (Revelation 3:17). Holy Spirit, come and move upon the Church in America with a spirit of conviction and repentance so that God's people will humble themselves and pray and seek Your face and turn from our wicked ways. And in Your gracious love and mercy, will You turn this nation from destruction, forgive our sin and heal our land (2 Chronicles 7:14)?

Most merciful God, forgive us for electing leaders who have supported legislation promoting death and perversion over life and righteousness. Forgive us for embracing political rhetoric over the unchanging Truth of Your Word. Forgive us for putting our hope in men instead of putting our hope in You. We call forth righteous, God-fearing patriotic statesmen/leaders who embrace the Founders' vision, support the Constitution and revere the Word of God.

We confess that, as a nation, we have denied and abandoned You and Your holy commandments. We have blasphemed Your Holy Name and deserve the consequences of our irreverent, rebellious behavior. O God of mercy, we are desperate for You! Oh, do not remember the former iniquities against us! In wrath remember mercy (Habakkuk. 3:2), for mercy triumphs over judgment (James 2:13). O Lord, Your mercies endure forever (Psalm136)!

Let Your tender mercies come speedily to meet us … .
Help us, O God of our salvation … .
For Your name's sake!
Why should the nations say, "Where is their God?"   Psalm 79:8-10

Will you not come and meet us (Psalm 59:10). Will You not REVIVE us once again, that Your people may rejoice in You (Psalm 85:6)?

Father, We pray for a mighty outpouring of Your Holy Spirit to bring forth REVIVAL and Reformation and a great harvest of souls into this land! May Your *River of Life* be released to counter the "culture of death" which has gripped this nation (Psalm 94:20-21). And may it spread to many cities across our land, to heal bodies and souls, transform hearts and set the captives free! We declare that the Blood of Jesus Christ has triumphed over and prevails against the spiritual hosts of wickedness aligned with Baal over this nation (Ephesians 6:12). For IT IS WRITTEN: "Having disarmed principalities and powers, Jesus made a public spectacle of them, triumphing over them through [the Blood of His cross]" (Colossians 2:15).

We stand in the authority of Isaiah 22:22 and close the doors of access used by the anti-Christ, humanistic structure that has infected our government and our society, and we declare a shifting to the foundation of TRUTH and RIGHTEOUSNESS at the gates of our nation. You are *Yahweh,* the God Who keeps covenant with His people. Lord, we bring You in remembrance of the blood of the martyrs upon this land … and of our godly heritage. Remember the faith of our founding fathers and their holy covenant with You for the dedication of this land to the glory of God and the furtherance to the Gospel. O, Lord, do not forget or forsake this covenant, we pray. For IT IS WRITTEN: "The scepter of wickedness shall not rest on the land allotted to the righteous" (Psalm 125:3). For the sake of Your mighty Name, do not allow our enemies to triumph over us!

We call the Church to AWAKE and ARISE! "Awake, awake you who sleep; come arise from the dead, and Christ will give you Light!" Arise and Shine to be the Light of the World you are called to be (Ephesians 5:14, Isaiah 60:1 and Matthew 5:14). IT IS WRITTEN that the gates of Hell shall not prevail against the Church. Mighty God, empower Your people to stand against the tide of evil that seeks to overwhelm us and to take this nation back for You. We call forth the "triumphant reserve" to stand in Apostolic alignment as the Kingdom-advancing, society-reforming governmental force You have called them to be. We cry out for this nation to be one that is exalted by righteousness (Proverbs 14:34) and whose God is the Lord (Psalm 33:12). We declare justice the measuring line and righteousness the plumbline over this nation (Isaiah 28:17-18). And we declare over America that the LORD is our Judge, the LORD is our Lawgiver, and the LORD is our King. HE will save us" (Isaiah 33:22)!

We speak to the gateways of our cities and our nation: "LIFT UP YOUR HEADS O YE GATES; AND BE LIFTED UP YE EVERLASTING DOORS, THAT THE KING OF GLORY MAY COME IN, the LORD STRONG AND MIGHTY, THE LORD MIGHTY IN BATTLE!" O LORD OF HOSTS (Psalm 24:7-10), arise in our midst so Your enemies will be scattered (Psalm 68:1). The heavens are Yours, and the earth also … . Righteousness and justice are the foundation of Your throne (Psalm 89:11 and 14). Establish the dominion of Your throne over our wayward nation.

AMERICA, ARISE TO YOUR DESTINY!

In the Name of Jesus and for His Glory!

PROCLAMATION OF REPENTANCE

Whereas: This nation has been a stiff-necked and rebellious people who have run after other gods, lusting after pleasures, money, fame and power.

Whereas: Sexual irresponsibility and perversion have polluted our nation, and the blood of the innocents cries out to You.

Whereas: We have embraced a "culture of death" where violence has permeated our entertainment, our homes and our schools.

Whereas: Our sins have destroyed lives, dishonored You and defiled our land.

Whereas: Many in the Church have profaned the holy Name of God by participating in and condoning the above sinful behavior.

And Whereas: IT IS WRITTEN:

IF MY PEOPLE, who are called by MY NAME, will humble themselves, and pray, and seek My face, and turn from their wicked ways, THEN I will hear from heaven, forgive their sin, and heal their land. 2 Chronicles 7:14

Most Gracious God, Creator of heaven and earth, Almighty in Power, Awesome in Grace and Mercy, the only True and Living God, we, Your people, humble ourselves before You this day and acknowledge that we have sinned greatly and deserve Your righteous wrath. We beseech You, our LORD, to remember the Blood of Jesus that was shed for us and, in wrath, to remember mercy. We implore You to pour out a Spirit of conviction and repentance upon your slumbering, backslidden Church so that all of God's people may truly humble themselves and pray and turn from their wicked ways.

We shamefully acknowledge, and humbly ask Your forgiveness, for:

- Our complacency, compromise and apathy.
- Loving the world more than God, which has made us Your enemies (James 4:4).
- Our ignorance of the Holy Scriptures and the life of Faith.
- Ignoring or neglecting our call to prayer and fasting.
- Living ungodly lifestyles that have profaned the Holy Name of the Lord (abortion, divorce, pornography and fornication are rampant in the Church).
- Clothing ourselves with affluence instead of the Lord Jesus Christ (Romans 13:11).
- The glorification of external beauty instead of the inner beauty of integrity and holiness (1 Peter 3:3-4).
- Being a part of the problem instead of the answer, not being salt and light.
- Harboring unforgiveness, bitterness, jealousy, hatred and offense toward our brothers.
- Having no holy fear of God. The fear of God is wisdom and the beginning of knowledge.
- Sleeping while the enemy has advanced his agendas across our land through our schools, our entertainment and false religion.
- Allowing this nation to plummet into the present depths of moral depravity (Job 28:28).
- Our lack of compassion for the lost, our failure to heed our Commission (Mark 16:15).
- Our lack of passion for the Lord and our idolatry, loving ourselves and the world more than Him.
- The anti-Semitic spirit which has pervaded the Church, and for the false belief that the Church has replaced Israel in God's prophetic and redemptive plan.
- Condoning homosexual "marriage" and leadership in the Church, calling acceptable and normal what God calls an abomination.

- The sins of racism and segregation.
- For embracing the wicked spirit of Freemasonry, which has brought deception and defilement upon the Church and this nation.
- For embracing political rhetoric over the unchanging truth of Your Word and voting in leaders who are promoting ungodly legislation, supporting death and perversion instead of life and righteousness.

O LORD, to us belongs shame of face because we have sinned against You. And so, gracious God, we make our prayer before You that we might turn from our iniquities and walk in Your truth. O LORD, according to all Your righteousness, we pray, let Your anger be turned away from our nation … . Righteous and merciful God, incline Your ear and hear; open Your eyes and see our desolations … for we do not present our supplications before You because of our righteous deeds, but because of Your great mercies. O Lord, hear! O Lord, forgive! O Lord, listen and act! Do not delay for Your own sake, my God … . For why should the nations say, 'Where is their God?' (Daniel 9 and Psalm 79:10).

O LORD, may You hear our prayers and supplications and forgive Your people who have sinned against You. Now, our God, we pray, let Your eyes be open and let Your ears be attentive to the prayers made today in this place. And may America once again be a nation which is exalted by righteousness and whose God is the LORD (Proverbs 14:34 and Psalm 33:12).

CALLING FORTH REVIVAL IN THE STATE OF MARYLAND

Agreeing with what the prophets Chuck Pierce and Dutch Sheets have spoken, we call forth the fire of God into our midst to restore our righteous foundation and to release that which has been dammed up ... . We proclaim "Womb be opened!" and "Seed awaken!" Let God's Kingdom come and His will be done in Maryland ... . We declare that this righteous shift in this state will cause the entire nation to be stirred for righteous change. We proclaim that Maryland is the state that "holds the line" against the onslaught of the homosexual agenda that has sought to redefine marriage and gender identity in this state. We declare: "Maryland, return to God! Return to worship your First Love!"

We call forth the Esthers to be positioned in spheres of societal and governmental influence. We call forth the Church to awaken and to shake off the reproach of idolatry and compromise and to come into the fullness of her destiny, unified as Christ's Kingdom Advancers!

Gracious Father of Light and Life, We pray for a mighty outpouring of Your Holy Spirit to bring forth REVIVAL and Reformation and a great harvest of souls into Maryland! May Your River of Life be released to counter the "culture of death" which has gripped this state. We declare that the Blood of Jesus Christ has triumphed over and continues to prevail against the spiritual hosts of wickedness aligned with Baal over this state (Ephesians 6:12). For IT IS WRITTEN: "Having disarmed principalities and powers, Jesus made a public spectacle of them, triumphing over them through (the blood of His cross)" (Colossians 2:15). And further, before the Court of the Almighty, the Ancient of Days (Daniel 7:9), we come into agreement with the decree on March 4, 2010 in our capital city of Annapolis, that this state of Maryland *has declared our divorcement from Baal and re-instated our holy marriage covenant with our God and King, Jesus Christ!* Therefore, in the Name of Jesus, let it be known this day that all covenants with death are annulled and this throne of iniquity, which devises evil law and condemns innocent blood, is brought down and stripped of all power (Psalm 94:20-21).

We further rebuke the spirits of insurrection and rebellion and declare Maryland is not, nor will ever be, a SANCTUARY STATE, nor will there ever be any SANCTUARY CITIES in the state of Maryland!

We stand in the governmental authority we have in Christ, seated with Him in heavenly places, and shut down the Gate of POWER and PER-VERSION that has controlled Maryland's destiny, and we RENAME THIS GOVERNMENTAL GATE **RIGHTEOUSNESS!**

RIGHTEOUSNESS EXALTS A NATION.   Proverbs 14:34

RIGHTEOUSNESS AND JUSTICE ARE THE FOUNDATION OF HIS THRONE.   Psalm 97:2

WE DECLARE:
The Maryland General Assembly shall no longer be manipulated by the power of men who seek to advance their own agendas. From this day forward, our legislators shall be governed by RIGHTEOUSNESS, advancing the agendas of Almighty God. His Word of Righteousness and Justice shall be your blueprint and His Spirit, your Counselor.

We speak to the entry ways of our state, the Eastern Gate of our nation: "Lift up your heads O ye gates, and be lifted up ye everlasting doors, that the KING OF GLORY may come in, the LORD strong and Mighty, the LORD mighty in battle (Psalm 24:7-10)! We welcome You, LORD OF HOSTS! The heavens are Yours and the earth also and all those who dwell therein (Psalm 24:1-3). We welcome You, KING OF GLORY! Righteousness and justice are the foundation of Your throne (Psalm 89:11 and 14). Establish the dominion of Your throne over Maryland. And let Your glory sweep across this nation from east to west. *In Jesus' Name and for His Glory*!

SPIRITUAL DECLARATIONS TO CLEANSE THE LAND

REPENTANCE:

If we confess our sins, He is faithful and just to forgive us our sins and to cleanse us from all unrighteousness.　　　　**1 John 1:9**

We stand on this land that has been defiled through sin and iniquity (Leviticus 18:24-26), **and we repent to our Great God** *whose mercies endure forever:*

- We repent over the **shedding of innocent blood** through warfare with First Nations Peoples and the enslavement of African Americans, and also because of blood shed through civil strife, gang violence, murder, addictions, family abuse and abortion. GOD HAVE MERCY!
- We repent over **broken covenants** with First Nations Peoples and ALL other people groups. We repent for adultery and broken marriages which end in divorce. GOD HAVE MERCY!
- We repent over **idolatry and false religion** — anything and everything we have put ahead of God, including the lust of the eyes, the lust of the flesh and the pride of life. GOD HAVE MERCY!
- We repent over **sexual sin** and **immorality** — homosexuality, fornication, pornography, human sex trafficking, adultery, fraud and bearing false witness. GOD HAVE MERCY!

PRAYERS (2 Chronicles 7:14):

(Inspired by prayers written by Randy and Barbara Walter of *Shiloh Ministries*)

- We pray that the Holy Spirit be fully released to operate unhindered in this community and its people, convicting them of righteousness, sin and judgment and leading them into all truth.

- We pray that the love of God will come in the power of the Holy Spirit, that the people of this community will be addicted to Jesus, righteousness and holiness instead of illicit drugs and lifestyles.
- We pray that a revelation of the goodness and love of God be poured out to set the captives free, and that those who have believed the devil's lies would receive their true identity as sons and daughters of their loving Father through the precious Blood of Jesus.
- We pray for the hearts of the parents to be turned to their children, the hearts of the children to be turned to their parents, and that *all hearts would be turned to the Lord.*
- We pray for wise and godly teachers and administrators who will teach our children biblical values and personal responsibility. We pray that the virtues of love, joy, peace, longsuffering, kindness, goodness, faithfulness, gentleness and self-control be displayed by students and staff alike.
- We pray for each child to know he has been uniquely created by and has great value to God, that children not be embarrassed, exploited, bullied, humiliated, shamed or devalued by peers or staff, and that the love of God would dislodge all forms of prejudice.
- We pray for the light of truth to expose all corruption and plots to bring harm to the citizens of this community.
- We pray for the protection of all law enforcement and EMS personnel and their families, spiritually, physically, mentally and emotionally.

DECLARATIONS (JOB 22:28):

Declarations to take back the Land....

We declare: "Lift up your heads you gates of this community! It is God's time for you! Your redemption draws near!" We declare that this community is open to the Gospel, open to salvation, and open to the Kingdom of God!

We declare that the people of this community have NO KING BUT JESUS! And He alone will be worshiped across our community!

We declare His Kingdom come and His will be done here as it is in heaven. We declare the dominion of His throne over our churches, our schools, our society and our families.

- We declare that the blood of Jesus covers this community and dislodges the spirits of anti-Christ and unbelief.
- We declare that the superior covenant which Jesus purchased with His own blood, that reconciles men to God, supersedes all unholy covenants.

We call for an end to the famine of God's Word in the churches in this community. Instead, we call our churches to be trumpeters of God's undiluted Word and worshipers in Spirit and truth.

We declare over the Church in this community: AWAKE! AWAKE, YOU WHO SLEEP! COME, ARISE FROM THE DEAD AND CHRIST WILL GIVE YOU LIGHT! YOU ARE THE LIGHT OF THE WORLD, SO, ARISE, SHINE, FOR YOUR LIGHT HAS COME, AND THE GLORY OF THE LORD HAS RISEN UPON YOU (Ephesians 5:14, Matthew 5:14 and Isaiah 60)!

We call the citizens of this community to awake from their slumber and support leaders who stand strong for biblical truth, righteousness and justice for all — *born and unborn*.

We call down the Goodness of God over this community which leads men to repentance.

We call forth an awakening to our youth to be transformed by the power of the cross.

- We call forth all gang members to have a life-changing encounter with the One True and Living God. We call them out of darkness and into the light.

- We say "NO!" to gang violence, terrorist cells, drug dealers, human traffickers, prostitution and all peddlers of corruption who operate or have influence in this community.
- We station guardian angels around our schools to protect them from all predators, especially sexual abusers and drug dealers, so that the neighborhoods around the schools are safe places to live and play.
- We call forth a fresh wind of the Holy Spirit to sweep out every hindering, perverse, deceptive and anti-Christ spirit out of our schools, and to usher in a revolution of holiness in our youth who will arise and shine with a contagious passion for Jesus and a love of the Truth.

We call forth a RETURN TO THE HOLY FEAR OF GOD that will restructure our society, restore our families, transform our schools, ignite revival fires throughout our community and bring life back to the land!

We declare that this community shall not die but live and declare the works of the Lord!

- In the name of Jesus, and because of the BLOOD of His cross, we take authority over the spirit of death in this community and declare that it has no power to keep people bound by fear, to deceive them into violence, to cause accidents or injuries, to inflict substance addiction or to produce premature death or suicide.
- We declare that in place of these things, God sends forth grace, peace, love, joy and knowledge of Himself, and that the love of Christ abounds to this community and overcomes all sins associated with the spirit of death.
- In the name of Jesus, we declare that the prince of the power of the air has no legal right to this community and cannot promote death through the airwaves, through the Internet or radio and TV broadcasting.
- In the name of Jesus, we take authority over and break the assignments of anger, hatred, prejudice, bitterness, jealousy, resentment, unforgiveness, greed, mental illness, depression and lawlessness in this community.

- We break every curse over this community and its people and pull down every vain imagination that would exalt itself against the knowledge of God.

We call forth this community to be a model community of peace, justice, compassion, charity, generosity and prosperity — in JESUS' NAME!

CHAPTER 7

FAMILIES AND CHILDREN

PROCLAIMING DESTINY
OVER OUR CHILDREN

TAKING AUTHORITY OVER DARKNESS:

We stand in the dominion we have been given by God and decree and declare a new day, a new season and a fresh anointing over our children. The ingredients of their destinies are programmed into their days, years and seasons. In the Name of Jesus, we bind every force that would attempt to capture their destinies illegitimately. We declare that the Blood of Jesus has prevailed against every principality, power, ruler of darkness and spiritual wickedness in high places assigned against the purposes of God for their lives.

We bind every destiny pirate, destiny thief and destiny devourer in the name of Jesus! We declare that they are dethroned and dismantled and have no influence over our children. Every curse sent against them is reversed and boomeranged back to the pits of hell. We declare that the control of the Luciferian spirit has been dismantled over their lives because of the Blood of Jesus. In the Name of Jesus, we bind every false light-bearer and counterfeit son of the morning, and we declare that our prayers are disrupting dark plans and causing failure to every enemy plan arrayed against our seed.

(Inspired by Dr. David Olukoya in his book, *Command the Morning*, www.mountain-of-fire.com)

SPEAKING LIFE AND LIGHT

Because of the redemptive, life-giving power of the Blood of Christ over their lives, we declare that the *strongman no longer has any right or authority to continue his rule in them.* We agree with Your Word that they are now delivered from the power of darkness and conveyed into the kingdom of LIGHT and the Son of Your love (Colossians 1:13). Therefore, we declare that the seat of authority in their hearts is possessed by the King of kings and Lord of lords. They are *blessed* because the ruling authority of God's Kingdom is established over and governs their lives. Therefore, nothing can separate them from the love of God (Romans 8:39), which is causing them to triumph and directing them to prosper. We declare that they are moving toward *advancement and destiny in Christ, and NO weapon formed against them shall succeed* (Isaiah 54:17)!

CALLING FORTH GOD'S BLESSINGS:

Father, we pray that from Your unlimited resources, goodness and riches You will empower and strengthen our children in their inner man with might through Your Spirit, and that Christ will dwell in their hearts through faith. We pray that You would impart to them revelation to understand the fullness of Your love and that they would be rooted and established in that love. May they each have a personal experience of the love of Christ that will transform their lives and their faith, so that they will be made complete in all the fullness of life and power that comes from God alone (Ephesians 3:14-19).

Father, we implore You to give them spiritual wisdom and revelation so that they might grow in the knowledge of God and know You more intimately. We pray that their hearts will be flooded with light so that they can understand the confident hope You have given to those You have called, and that they would understand and access all the treasures of their inheritance stored up in the heavenly realm (Colossians 1:5). We pray that You would baptize them in Your Holy Spirit and Fire, so that they can do the works that Jesus did and be a part of the End-Times Army You are raising up to advance Your Kingdom in the earth. We pray that they will understand the incomparable greatness of God's resurrection power available to us who believe in Him, that mighty power that raised Christ from the dead and seated him in the place of honor at God's right hand in the heavenly realms.

Father, we pray that they would understand that through Christ they, too, are seated with Him in the Heavenly places. And, from that positioning in Him, may they discover the path to fulfill their destinies, laid out before time began (Ephesians 1:16-20, Matthew 3:11 and 2 Timothy 1:9)!

PRAYER FOR THE RESTORATION OF FAMILIES

Father, You have established the family unit as the backbone of society. So I call forth the restoration of our families to the biblical model. Lord, bring Your holy alignment into our fractured families. Bring back the prodigal fathers to take their places as the priests of their homes, so that they would not provoke their children to anger, but bring them up in "the training and admonition of the Lord" (Ephesians 6:4). And I call forth mothers to adhere to their holy calling and forsake the lure of the marketplace and the business world. Let them hear the heart cries of their children and be the nurturers that their children need.

Gracious Father, turn the hearts of the fathers (and mothers) to the children and the children to the fathers (and mothers) (Malachi 4:6), so that children will honor and obey their parents according to the admonition of your Word (Ephesians 6:1-2). I call forth biblical marriages where husbands love and cherish their wives as Christ loves the Church and wives honor and submit to their husbands as unto the Lord (Ephesians 5:22 and 5). Under this holy alignment, may husbands and wives submit to one another in mutual compassion and humility (Ephesians 5:12 and 1 Peter 3:8).

In the Name of Jesus, I call men and women return to their natural affections (1 Timothy 3:3), and I rebuke the spirits of perversion that seek to redefine the American family. May the covenant of marriage be honored by all and the marriage bed undefiled, in Jesus' name (Hebrews 13:4)!

PRAYER FOR SALVATION

Father, we lift these people before You and ask You to fill their lives with Your Outrageous Grace, that they might have life-changing encounters with the Living God (Romans 5:20). We call forth angels to position them to receive Your magnanimous Love, so that Christ may dwell in their hearts through faith (Ephesians 3:17). We pray that Light would flood their darkened minds (Ephesians 1:18), so that they would be filled with all the fullness of God and the knowledge of His will in all wisdom and spiritual understanding (Ephesians 3:19 and Colossians 1:9). We ask You, Father, to qualify them to be partakers of the inheritance of the saints in the Light and to deliver them from the power of darkness. We declare over them: "In the Name of Jesus Christ, your sins are forgiven." [2] We proclaim the Redemptive, life-giving power of the Blood of Christ over their lives as You, Father, establish them in Your Kingdom (Colossians 1:12-14) and overwhelm them with Your love.

---

2. We all know people who, no matter what biblical truth is told them, are *unwilling* or *unable* to receive it. When people are surrounded by an atmosphere of sin (created by unforgiveness), there is a barrier around them that is keeping *all truth and light out and darkness and lies in.* Satan then has legal authority over them and their lives. On the other hand, **forgiveness changes the legal spiritual atmosphere over people** where satan has ruled and **allows them to see and hear the truth from** God. So, when we speak over a person in such bondage, **"In the Name of Jesus Christ, your sins are forgiven you,"** the authority that satan has moved in to keep them in bondage to lies is now broken and removed. This has nothing to do with salvation. It has to do with loosing people from bondages *so that they can be saved. (Insights from Dr. Yolanda McCune, Heartland Apostolic Prayer Network).*

DELIVERANCE PROCLAMATION OVER THE SPIRIT MAN
(TO ARISE TO HIS TRUE IDENTITY AND DESTINY)

HOLY FATHER,

Your Word says that those who were dead and in darkness and sin, You made alive ... . So we call forth _____ to be released from the *energy of disobedience,* set free from *the power and energy of this age,* and set free from *the satanic energy* that produces disobedience and unbelief. We say, _____, "Your sins are forgiven you." The Blood of Jesus has prevailed on your behalf, and you are now set free to hear the Truth of who you really are in Christ as the Beloved of God.

Father, because of Your great mercy, grace and love, loose him once and for all from the influence of the prince of the power of the air, and release him in Your **resurrection power** to *make him alive. Raise him up* out of darkness and into the light of your eternal Kingdom where he is seated with Christ in heavenly places (Ephesians 2:1-6).

TO THE ONE CAUGHT IN BONDAGE,

We speak to your spirit man and bring you in remembrance of the Father's blueprint of love and overcoming victory that is stamped on your spiritual DNA.

We bless your spirit with strength to rise up in overcoming power against the root of iniquity and spiritual poverty in your generational blood line. The spirits of addiction and the lusts of the flesh are broken over you in Jesus' name and by the power of **His shed Blood.**

So, **we call you out of bondage and into freedom**, out of darkness and into light, out of poverty and into your riches in Christ, Who has given you all things that pertain to life and godliness (2 Peter 1:3).

We call your spirit to transform your behavior as you discover your *triumphal, ascended identity in Christ.*

We call your spirit to reach out and embrace your God, Your Father, Who loves you, Jesus Who died for you, the Holy Spirit, your Teacher, counselor, strength and shield. *Embrace truth! Embrace righteousness! Embrace victory, healing and redemption that are yours in Christ!*

For Your Father "has delivered you from the power of darkness and conveyed you into the Kingdom of the Son of His love, in whom you have redemption through His Blood, the forgiveness of sins" (Colossians 1:13).

THE MARRIAGE BLESSING
(TO BE IMPARTED OVER MARRIED COUPLES)

- Unconditional love reigns supreme in your life because the love of God is shed abroad in your hearts by the Holy Spirit (Romans 5:5).
- Your love is patient and kind. It does not envy or boast. It is not rude, self-seeking or easily angered. It does not delight in evil, but rejoices in the truth. It will always protect, always trust, always hope and always persevere. Your love will never fail (1 Corinthians 13:4-8).
- You will be imitators of God, living a life of love, in humility, esteeming each other as better than yourself (Ephesians 5:1 and Philippians 2:3).
- You will submit to one another out of reverence to Christ (Ephesians 5:21). The wife will submit to and honor the husband as unto the Lord. The husband will love his wife as Christ loves the church and gave Himself for her (Ephesians 5:22 and 25).
- You are together, united with Christ, like-minded, having the same love, being one in spirit and purpose (Philippians 2:2).
- What God has joined together, neither man nor demon will separate (Mark 10:8).

DAILY BLESSING PRAYER

I pray for you, my friend, today:

- That you may be filled with all the fullness of God and the knowledge of His will in all wisdom and spiritual understanding.
- That you may walk worthy of the Lord, fully pleasing *Him,* being fruitful in every good work and increasing in the knowledge of God.
- That you may be strengthened with all might, according to His glorious power in your inner man, having patience and longsuffering with joy.
- That you may have a thankful heart, giving thanks to the Father who has qualified you to be a partaker of the inheritance of the saints in the light (Colossians 1:9-13).
- That God would grant you, according to the riches of His glory, to be strengthened with might through His Spirit in your inner being.
- That you, being rooted and grounded in love, may be able to experience the width and length and depth and height of God's love, which passes knowledge.
- That you may be filled with all the fullness of God (Ephesians 3:16-19).
- That you are blessed and highly favored of God. His favor surrounds you like a shield (Psalm 5:12)!
- That the comforts of *Jehovah Shalom* delight your soul as anxieties rise within you (Psalm 94:19).

May our wonderful God give to you this day **the spirit of wisdom and revelation in the knowledge of Him,** opening the eyes of your understanding to know:

- What is the hope of His calling.
- What are the riches of the glory of His inheritance in the saints.
- What *is* the **exceeding greatness** of His power toward us who believe (Ephesians 1:16-19).

I declare over you the **finished work** of the cross, to bring you into *Covenant Wholeness* in mind, body and spirit (Isaiah 53:4-5).

AND I release all the **power of the Resurrection** (Ephesians 1:19-20) into your life, that you might live and minister in the power of the Kingdom and fulfill your God-ordained destiny in Christ.

May you go forth this day in the **victory** that Christ died to give you!

PROCLAMATION OF FAITH FOR SAFETY AND PROTECTION (FROM PSALM 91)

Psalm 91 is a powerful confession concerning safety and protection. The following version is a paraphrased and annotated adaptation from my book, "Praying with Authority and Power." Filled with promises of God's sovereign protection, I call it God's "Life *Assurance* Policy."

A PERSONAL CONFESSION OF FAITH FOR SAFETY AND PROTECTION

God's Life Assurance Policy

Because we dwell in the secret place of the Most High, we abide under the shadow of the Almighty. We declare of the Lord, "He is our refuge and our fortress; our God, in Him we will trust." For surely He shall deliver us from the spiritual traps of the enemy and from the perils of life-threatening weapons of natural war. He shall cover us with His protection, and under His sovereign care we shall take refuge. His truth shall be our shield and defense. *And His Word our sword* (Ephesians 6:17).

We shall not be afraid of the terror by night, nor of the missiles that fly by day, nor of biological or nuclear warfare. *We have no fear because God has given us a spirit of power, of love, and a sound mind* (2 Timothy 1:7). A thousand may fall at our side, and ten thousand at our right hand; but it shall not come near us. *For no weapon formed against us shall prosper* (Isaiah 54:17). The wicked will only *appear* to be winning.

Because we have made the Lord, who is our refuge, even the Most High, our dwelling place, no evil shall befall us, nor shall any plague come near our dwelling. For He shall give His angels charge over us, to keep us in all our ways. In their hands they shall bear us up, lest we stumble and fall. We have authority to render ineffective all the strategies of destruction of the enemy. *For God has given us authority over ALL his power* (Luke 10:19).

Because we have set our love on Him, He will deliver us; He will set us on high because we have known Him personally. *He honors His Blood Covenant with us* (1 Corinthians 11:25). We shall call upon Him, and He will answer us; He will be with us in trouble; He will deliver us and honor us. *His plans for us are for good, to give us hope and a sure future* (Jeremiah 29:11). With long life He will satisfy us and show us His salvation.

PRAYING FOR OUR SCHOOLS AND OUR CHILDREN

The enemy is after this generation. From gender confusion and homosexuality to abortion, drugs and gang-related violence, our children have become prime targets for destruction. And the level of gun violence and terror attacks in schools has risen alarmingly. But we are seated governmentally with Christ and carry His authority in the earth realm. We must be proactive in our prayers and take the offensive position! Our children have God-ordained destinies to fulfill!

Whoever causes one of these little ones who believe in Me to sin, it would be better for him if a millstone were hung around his neck, and he were drowned in the depth of the sea. Matthew 18:6

IN THE NAME OF JESUS,

WE REPENT for school teachers and administrators who would lead our children astray into false anti-biblical belief systems. We pray that God would turn their hearts from evil and give them a revelation of Truth.

WE CALL FORTH LIFE:
- May God-fearing teachers raise up **curricula which will nurture young people of biblical integrity and moral character**.
- May a fresh wind of the Holy Spirit **sweep every hindering, perverse, unclean, deceptive and anti-Christ spirit out of our schools**.

WE DRIVE THE DARKNESS OUT: We **plead the Blood of Jesus** over our schools and children and declare that His Blood has triumphed over, and continues to prevail against all works of the enemy (Colossians 2:15).

We forbid any demonically-motivated violence to invade our schools, rec centers, ball fields and any places where youth gather.

We Declare that no weapon formed against our youth shall prosper (Isaiah 54:17).

We Bind the culture of death which has permeated the lives of our youth through movies, videos, the Internet and social media, inciting acts of violence and murder. We also bind the orphan spirit and spirits of abandonment and abuse suffered by many children in dysfunctional families.

WE CALL FORTH:

- Families which **nurture children in love** and teach and model biblical principals.
- A generation of youth that embraces a **revolution of holiness** and arises with a **contagious passion for Jesus** and a **love of the Truth.**

WE ASK GOD TO:

- **Send His guardian angels** to surround our schools, to protect them from all predators, especially traffickers and drug dealers, so that our schools and neighborhoods are safe places to live and play.
- **Expose and intercept** all evil plots to bring terror and destruction to our schools and our children.
- **Guard our children** from gender confusion and sexual exploitation. Help every child to know his value to God and his true identity in Christ as a child of God.

WE INVITE GOD'S LOVE AND REVIVAL TO COME:

- **To surround them with His love** (Colossians 1:9-12).
- **To fill them with the knowledge** of His will and the knowledge of God through the power of the Holy Spirit, so that they may live a life pleasing to God, bearing the fruit of good works.

- **Strengthen them with all power** according to His glorious might, so that they may have great endurance, patience and thankfulness.
- **Rescue them from the dominion of darkness** and bring them into the Kingdom of light, in which they have redemption through the Blood of Christ.

OH GOD, **Will You not revive us again,**
That Your people may rejoice in You?
Show us Your mercy, Lord,
And grant us Your salvation.　　　　　　　　　　Psalm 85:6-7

CHAPTER 8

HEALTH AND HEALING

DECLARING HEALTH FROM A KINGDOM PERSPECTIVE

My body MUST come into alignment with the *Kingdom government* that I carry in Christ — NO infirmity, only wholeness and completeness (Colossians 2:9-10 and Galatians 2:20).

- As I have died with Christ, I have also *ascended with Him* into the Heavenly realm of perfection (Colossians 3:1-4 and Romans 6:4-5).
- I am not subject to the curse of sin and death, but subject to the spirit of *abundant life* in Christ Jesus (Galatians 3:13, Romans 8:2, and John 5:24 and 10:10).
- Creation MUST respond to the *Glory of Heaven* that is within me (Colossians 3:4 and Romans 8:30).
- My physical body is taking on incorruption (2 Corinthians 3:18 and 1 Corinthians 15:42-50) because it is continually being quickened by the *Resurrection Life of Christ* within me (Romans 8:11 and John 11:25-26).

*Christ's resurrection from the dead is my resurrection too. This is why I yearn for all that is above, for that is where Christ sits enthroned at the place of all power, honor and authority! Yes, I feast on all the treasures of the heavenly realm and fill my thoughts with heavenly realities, and not with the distractions of the natural realm. My crucifixion with Christ has severed the tie to this life, and now my true life is hidden away in God as I live within the Anointed One. Every time Christ Himself is seen for Who He really is, who I really am will also be revealed, for I am now ONE with Him in His Glory! So I consider my life in this natural realm as already dead and buried! ... And **I live as one who has died to disease** (Colossians 3:1-5, The Passion Bible).* [3]

---

3. The Passion Translation® Copyright © 2017 by BroadStreet Publishing® Group, LLC.

DECLARING TRUTH FOR OPTIMAL HEALTH

Those who live in the shelter of the Most High
will find **rest in the shadow of the Almighty.**
This I declare about the LORD:
He alone is my refuge, my place of safety;
he is my God, and I trust him.
For **he will rescue me from every trap**
and protect me from deadly disease.
He will cover me with his feathers.
He will shelter me with his wings.
His faithful promises are my armor and protection.

Psalm 91:1-5

THEREFORE, IT IS WRITTEN:

* **Jesus, the Healer lives in me,** and so all the fullness of Divine health fills every cell of my being (Galatians 2:20).
* I have wholeness of mind, spirit and BODY because Jesus took upon Himself my sins and sicknesses on the cross of Calvary, and **by His stripes I am healed** (Isaiah 53:5-6)!
* When Jesus was resurrected to new life, I was too, and so **I live as one who has died to diseases** (Colossians 3:1-5, The Passion Bible)!

"Christ's resurrection from the dead is your resurrection too. This is why we are to yearn for all that is above, for that's where Christ sits enthroned at the place of all power, honor and authority! Yes, feast on all the treasures of the heavenly realm and fill your thoughts with heavenly realities, and not with the distractions of the natural realm. Our crucifixion with Christ has severed the tie to this life, and now your true life is hidden away in God as you live within the Anointed One .... So consider your life in this natural realm as already dead and buried ... and live as one who has died to diseases ...."

- God's plans for me are for good, to give me hope and a future. He has spoken things over my life which have not yet come to pass. **I have a destiny to fulfill** (Jeremiah 29:11)!
- I am counting it all JOY because God is perfecting faith in me, to believe that He causes me to triumph in every situation (James 1:2 and 1 Corinthians 15:57). **The greater the trial, the greater the victory!**
- **I am more than a conqueror** because of my identity in Christ (Romans 8:37). As He has overcome, so I shall overcome! I choose to see this test as another opportunity to overcome (John 16:33).
- I am not living under the circumstances of this world but **am seated victoriously with Christ in heavenly places where there is NO sickness** (Ephesians 2:6). Therefore, I choose a *triumphal* life perspective and see victory in every situation. *I am resting in a place of victory, not fighting toward it.* Thanks be to God Who ALWAYS leads me to TRIUMPH IN CHRIST (2 Corinthians 2:14)!
- **God is working all things in my life for good,** so I choose to believe that God is using this circumstance to make me look more like HIM (Romans 8:28).
- **My body (DNA) is being transformed, to become a resurrection body where no sickness can abide.**

For our citizenship is in heaven, from which we also eagerly wait for the Savior, the Lord Jesus Christ, who will **transform our lowly body that it may be conformed to His glorious body,** *according to the working by which He is able even to subdue all things to Himself.*

Philippians 3:20-21

For the same spirit that raised Christ from the dead lives in me and is quickening my mortal body.　　　　Romans 8:11

- The cross defeated the curse that came as a result of Adam's sin and opened to me a whole new realm of living (Romans 8:2). Therefore I am not subject to the curse of sin and death, but **subject to the** spirit of **ABUNDANT LIFE in Christ Jesus** (Galatians 3:13, John 10:10 and Romans 8:2).

- **As He is, so am I in this world** (1 John 4:17) — beautiful, powerful, anointed, prophetic, wise, strong, overcoming, victorious and full of life!
- This situation is bringing **empowerment and upgrade into my life** because I am joyfully vulnerable to God's ability in the midst of my difficulties (2 Timothy 2:1:12).

I CHOOSE TO TAKE GOD AT HIS WORD AND TO COMPLETELY TRUST IN HIS GOODNESS AND LOVE FOR ME IN THIS AND EVERY CIRCUMSTANCE.

This trial is but a **doorway to the Kingdom.** I have a victory mentality and embrace this trial as **an opportunity for a greater victory and Kingdom advancement!**

So, I am resting in the finished work of Christ and standing on these foundational TRUTHS, which supersede all circumstances and FACTS.

And now, O LORD, the Word which You have spoken concerning your servant, ESTABLISH IT FOREVER AND DO AS THOU HAST SAID!   2 Samuel 7:25

The Kingdom of Heaven is at hand!   Matthew 10:7

(As Jesus brought the Kingdom to earth, miracles, signs and wonders were released.)

DECLARATION OF FAITH FOR HEALING ACCORDING TO THE WORD OF GOD

(This declaration names the diseases of Alzheimer's and dementia, but it can be adapted to *any* illness or disease)

Our gracious Father, infinite in love and power, we hold _____ before Your throne of grace, that You told us to approach confidently in our time of need (Hebrews 4:16), and we confess Your Word concerning healing. We declare that IT IS WRITTEN.

_____ is a blood-covenant child of Yours, and so no weapon formed against him shall prosper (Isaiah 54:17). _____ is redeemed from the curse of the Law (of which sickness is a part), because Jesus bore his sicknesses and carried his diseases in His own body (Galatians 3:13), and by His stripes _____ is healed (Isaiah 53:4 and Matthew 8:17). Therefore we forbid any infirmity or disease to operate in _____'s body. We rebuke the spirit of Dementia and Alzheimer's and all mental confusion and deterioration associated with those names. And we declare that the Name of JESUS is situated in supreme authority over every other name, and at His Name Dementia/Alzheimer's must bow, cease and desist its operations against _____ (Philippians 2:9-10). We call every organ and tissue in _____'s body, specifically those involved with hearing, vision and cognitive ability, to function in the perfection in which God created them to function. For _____ is fearfully and wonderfully made.

Lord, we pray that _____ would be allowed to complete every day of his life and fulfill completely his destiny in Christ which You spoke over him before he was even born (Psalm 139:14-16). Thank You, Father, for the assurance of Your Word that the angel of the Lord encamps around _____ and delivers him from every evil work (Psalm 34:7). Therefore, no evil shall befall him; nor plague nor calamity shall be allowed to prosper over him (Psalm 91:10-11).

We declare over _____ that the Word of God abides in him and delivers to him perfect soundness of mind and wholeness of body and spirit from the deepest parts of his nature in his immortal spirit even to the joints and marrow of his bones. That Word is medication and life to his flesh (Proverbs 4:22), for the law of the Spirit of life operates in him and makes him free from the law of sin and death (Romans 8:2). And since the same Spirit that raised Christ from the dead dwells in _____, the life-giving power of that Spirit is also quickening his mortal body (Romans 8:11).

Satan, we speak to you in the name and authority of Jesus Christ (John 14:14 and 16:23) and say that the Blood of the Lamb of God has triumphed over and continues to prevail against you on _____'s behalf (Colossians 2:15). For he is the property of Almighty God, and we give you no place in him. We declare that _____ dwells in the secret place, the refuge and fortress, of the Most High God, and that he remains stable and fixed under the shadow of the Almighty, *whose power no foe can withstand* (Psalm 91:1-2).

We lay hold of faith, standing immovable and fixed in full assurance, that _____ has health and healing now, according to Your covenant promises to him as a blood-bought child of Almighty God (Mark 11:22-24).[4]

---

4. Inspired by "Health and Healing," page 67, *Prayers that Avail Much*, Word Ministries, Inc.

MY DECREE OF LIFE

When the enemy makes a decree of death over you, this is your response:

In the Name of my King, Jesus Christ, the Most High God, I reverse the decree of death the enemy has made against me. He is defeated by the Blood of the Lamb and has no authority in my life. I have wholeness of mind, body and spirit because Jesus took upon Himself my sins and sicknesses on the cross of Calvary, and by His stripes I am healed. Therefore I declare in counter decree, in *the Name that is above all other names*, JESUS CHRIST my Lord, that all the plans and actions of the devil that are arrayed against me are null and void according to the Blood Covenant I have with Almighty God.

IT IS WRITTEN: No weapon formed against me shall prosper, and every tongue that rises up against me in judgment I shall condemn. **My God has declared Kingdom (abundant) life over me.** I shall live and not die and praise the wonderful works of God … . I shall continue to bear fruit in old age … . I shall be fresh and flourishing. Therefore I shall fulfill completely my destiny and calling in Christ that was spoken over my life before the world began, for the ruling authority of God's Kingdom is established over and governs my life (Colossians 2:15; Isaiah 53:5 and 4:17; John 10:10; Psalms 118:17, 92:12-14 and 139:16).

LIFE DECREE (OVER CANCER)

IN THE NAME OF JESUS we rebuke the spirit of death off of _____, and we speak ABUNDANT LIFE to take that place. Jesus said: "I have come that they might have LIFE and have it *more abundantly.*" So we call _____'s body into agreement and alignment with the LIFE decree of Jesus! Therefore, we call his/her body into alignment with the TRUTH of the Word of God.

Jesus, the Healer, lives in _____ (Galatians 2:20). Therefore, the Kingdom, in all the fullness of Divine health, saturates his/her being, so that sickness may not prosper in his/her body. Furthermore, God's Words are life to those who find them and health to all their flesh (Proverbs 4:22), and they have creative power in _____'s body to bring forth what they say (Romans 4:21). Therefore, as IT IS WRITTEN, by the stripes of Jesus _____ was healed 2000 years ago (Isaiah 53:4-5). **Jesus has paid the price for** _____**'s healing!** And so we call forth the creative power of the Truth of God's Words of life to explode in _____'s body to eradicate every cancer cell. We declare that _____ shall live out fully every day of his/her life that God has written in His book for him/her (Psalm 139:16). And we proclaim: he/she shall live and not die and declare the wondrous works of the Lord (Psalm 118:17)! Amen!

TRUTH PRESCRIPTION FOR HEALING
*(TO BE DECLARED AS **MEDICINE TO***
***YOUR SPIRIT AND SOUL** WHENEVER YOU*
TAKE MEDICINE FOR YOUR BODY)

Gracious Abba Father, thank You that Jesus, the Healer, lives in me! Therefore, the Kingdom, in all the fullness of Divine health, saturates my being so that sickness may not prosper in my body. Furthermore, Your words are LIFE to those who find them and HEALTH to all their flesh (Proverbs 4:22). I believe with Abraham that **Your Word has creative power in my body to bring forth what it says** (Romans 4:21). Therefore, AS IT IS WRITTEN, **by the stripes of Jesus *I am healed*!** So I am not looking ahead to a time when *I will* be healed. I am looking *back* to the time I WAS healed, 2000 years ago (Isaiah 53:5)!

So, Father, I ask that the CREATIVE POWER of the **Truth** of Your Words would explode in my body, to eradicate any sickness or any remaining diseased or damaged cells, so that I shall live and declare the wondrous works of the Lord (Psalm 118:17)!

CHAPTER 9

COMMUNION

INTRODUCTION TO COMMUNION PRAYER

In the fullest understanding, Communion celebrates the Triumph of the Kingdom to restore all that was lost as a result of Adam's sin.

Jesus emphasizes the power of Communion to transfigure life:

I am the bread of life. Your fathers ate the manna in the wilderness, and are dead. This is the bread which comes down from heaven, that one may eat of it and **not die***. I am the living bread which came down from heaven. If anyone eats of this bread, he will* **live forever;** *.... . Most assuredly, I say to you, unless you eat the flesh of the Son of Man and drink His blood, you have no life in you. Whoever* **eats My flesh and drinks My blood** *has eternal life, and I will raise him up at the last day.* ["Eats" in this verse in the Greek is "trogo." It means "to chew or gnaw with crunching sound." This is not merely a spiritual, but a physical experience.] *For* **My flesh is food indeed, and My blood is drink indeed.** *He who eats My flesh and drinks My blood abides in Me, and I in him. As the living Father sent Me, and I live because of the Father, so he who feeds on Me* **will live** *because of Me. This is the bread which came down from heaven—not as your fathers ate the manna, and are dead. He who eats this bread* **will live forever.** *"*
John 6:48-58

Four times Jesus said WILL LIVE or NOT DIE.

Dr. Brian Simmons, the translator of *The Passion Translation*, says this about the above passage: "This 'eating' and 'drinking' is receiving the life, power, and virtue of **ALL that Jesus is** (**"New man,"** Romans 6:4 and Ephesians 4:22-24), to replace **all that we were in Adam** (**"old man"**). **Jesus' Blood and Body is the TREE of LIFE** which is offered to everyone who follows Him" (see Genesis 3:22-24, where Adam and Eve were cut off from the Tree of Life lest they *eat and live forever).*

Colossians 2:14 in The Passion Bible says: *"And through the Divine authority of His cross, He canceled out every legal violation we had on our record … that stood to indict us. He erased it ALL – our sins, **our stained soul** [and our shameful failure to keep His laws] – He deleted it all and it cannot be retrieved! Everything **we were in Adam has** been placed onto His cross and nailed permanently there as a public display of cancellation."*
Dr. Simmons says this about the phrases above in boldface: "This would mean the DNA of Adam has been erased **and the DNA of Christ has been embedded into us through the cross and resurrection life of Christ."**

- We are new creatures in Christ (2 Corinthians 5:1, Philippians 3:20 and Romans 8:23).
- All the fullness of the Godhead is in Christ, and, therefore, in us (John 14 and Colossians 2:9).

Why then do we need to receive the life/DNA of Christ through Communion? Christ-likeness is a *process of becoming transformed.*

But we all, with unveiled face, beholding as in a mirror the glory of the Lord, **are being transformed into the same image from glory to glory,** *just as by the Spirit of the Lord.* 2 Corinthians 3:18

We need **to be renewed in the "spirit"** [perception, desires] **of our minds** (Ephesians 4: 22-24). And, we must BELIEVE. In John 11:21-25, Martha was talking to Jesus about her brother Lazarus:

Jesus told her, "Your brother will rise and live."
She replied, "Yes I know he will rise with everyone else on resurrection day."
"Martha," Jesus said, "you don't have to wait until then. **I AM the RESURRECTION, and I AM LIFE ETERNAL.** *Anyone who clings to Me in faith, even though he dies, will live forever. And* **the one who**

lives by believing in Me *will NEVER die.* [5] *Do you believe this?*" (The Passion Translation)

So there are two groups of people in this passage:
1. One that will die and *then live forever*
2. One that will live and *believe and never die*

The bottom line is this: **You will be what you believe.** If you believe that you will die like generations before you, then you will die in the body you were born in. BUT if you BELIEVE and confess and appropriate by faith through Communion that you will not die, **then you will not die.**

Having said all of this, this is not just about by-passing death. It is about *receiving the fullness of ALL that Christ died to give us.* It is about taking on CHRIST-LIKENESS. As we are **transformed into His image from glory to glory, *our entire being will be affected.*** So, as we renew our minds, behold His glory and receive by faith the Body and Blood of Christ, **we believe we are *being transformed TOTALLY — mind, spirit and body.***

At this time, Heaven is more accessible than it has ever been. Realms of glory are opening to us that previously only ones like Enoch and Elijah engaged. Let's step through in faith and engage the heavenly NOW!

---

5. Will NEVER die: Dr. Simmon's footnote here says that the Greek is VERY emphatic in this statement. It literally means "will never die FOREVER."

PERSONAL COMMUNION PRAYER
(Celebrating the Triumph of His Kingdom, Beholding His Glory)

Worthy is the Lamb that was slain to receive power and riches and wisdom and strength and honor and glory and blessing!
Revelation 5:12

At this time, Heaven is more accessible than it has ever been. Realms of Glory are opening to us that previously only ones like Enoch and Elijah engaged. Jesus commanded us to abide in Him by eating His flesh and drinking His blood, and *so live a life that will never die* (John 6:51-57). **For *His Body carries the record of His transfiguration and His Blood carries the DNA of our Father*.** Even though our DNA is flawed, Communion is changing that record by **imparting the very Life of God** that will **transfigure us *into His Glory Blueprint that has been embedded in us*** (Colossians1:27 and Philippians 3:20). We choose to engage in the DNA of God, our Father. And it is our faith declaration that as we receive this Communion, we are receiving God's restoring, transforming and healing LIFE – *Life that will never die.* We celebrate Jesus' atoning sacrifice and our glorious Redemption, which included the defeat of all works of sin and the demonic world (Colossians 2:13-15), and we look *forward* to our becoming *full sons* in the Kingdom of our Father (Romans 8:18-19), **which includes our physical bodies being transformed** (Romans 8:23, *The Passion Translation*).

Therefore, Yeshua, Our Mighty Redeemer, with holy reverence we remember and thank You for Your suffering on our behalf, which has expunged our sin. And with grateful hearts we receive ALL of the KINGDOM benefits of Your holy sacrifice, which have brought us into our **new identity in Christ** and a **new life of hope and victory.** And so, by faith, we receive this physical food as spiritual food to our bodies that will bring *transfiguration at the cellular level.*

As we have communion with Your Spirit, we ask You to forgive us and cleanse us from all unrighteousness and to build the resurrected Christ in us. **Jesus, You are the Bread of Life and the TREE of LIFE** (John 6:48). As we receive, by faith, Your Body and Your Blood, we thank You that *in the very cellular structure of our physical bodies we are being transfigured* — from glory to glory — into radiant creative light beings like You (Philippians 3:20-21 and 2 Corinthians 3:18).

WITH THIS BREAD, YOUR BODY (THE BREAD OF LIFE):
We receive the power of Your abundant, eternal life abiding in us (John 6:50-51 and 56 and 10:10). We receive all the fullness of Who You are, Christ in us, the hope of glory (Colossians 1:27). Help us to take up our cross daily and die to self (Matthew 16:24 and 10:38), so that the fullness of Your life and Person may be manifested through our lives in increasingly greater measure, until we are walking in the fullness of the KINGDOM realm on earth as it is in Heaven. We eat healing power for our bodies and proclaim the finished work of the cross (John 19:30) to be effective in us, to bring us *Covenant wholeness.* By Your stripes we are healed — mind, body and spirit (Isaiah 53:4-5). We call our bodies into alignment with the Kingdom government that we carry, Your Covenant design in Isaiah 53, *and with the record of Your indwelling Transfiguration.* We shall be fresh and flourishing and fruit-bearing throughout our life on earth (Psalm 92:14) and continuing into Eternity. **So, as we eat this bread, Lord, we partake of the TREE of LIFE, and we thank You for Eternal, KINGDOM Resurrection life through Your body** (John 6:48-51 and Revelation 5:12).

WITH THIS CUP OF THE NEW COVENANT IN YOUR BLOOD
(THE CUP OF VICTORY):
We drink and proclaim redemption for our souls. We drink the power of forgiveness and receive the release that it brings. We drink of the power that sets the captives free. We declare complete victory over the enemy, and we receive deliverance and cleansing from the guilt and power of sin and all of its destructive fruit, including sickness and disease (Hebrews 9:12-14).

Through Your precious Blood, **we receive the perfect DNA of our Father** and the empowerment of *Divine Life Energy* from the Resurrection, because the same Spirit that raised Christ from the dead is now quickening our mortal bodies (Romans 8:11). And so we drink of the power of the Blood to *seal our redemption, our healing, and power to overcome every spiritual enemy and every earthly constraint.* **So, as we drink this cup, Lord, we thank You for the KINGDOM victory in Your Blood** (Revelation 12:11).

THE CONCLUSION, A RESURRECTION PROCLAMATION

When Jesus was resurrected to new life, so were we. So we now appropriate the fullness of the Resurrection with these declarations from Ephesians 1:19-20. **May all the Power of Your Kingdom through Your Resurrection be manifested in our lives** for Your glory! **Help us to walk in the *dunamis* (miracle-working) power available to us who believe:**

- May Your *energia* power make effective the operation of the gifts of the Spirit — with signs, wonders and miracles — that we might more effectively reveal Your Kingdom in this world.
- May Your *ischuos* muscle power deliver us from all that is carnal and unclean and empower us to prevail in and overcome every demand and challenge.
- May the *kratos* power of Your government help us to be strong in the Lord and in the power of Your might, establishing the dominion of Your throne over our lives!

CELEBRATING COMMUNION IN PREPARATION FOR WARFARE

(Celebrating the Triumph of His Kingdom, Beholding His Glory)

Worthy is the Lamb that was slain to receive power and riches and wisdom and strength and honor and glory and blessing!
Revelation 5:12

Jesus said, in John 6:48-58, that His body is REAL food and His Blood is REAL drink, and that as we receive His Body and Blood, we are receiving the very LIFE of GOD, life that will never die. So we celebrate His (and our) victory as we receive His Body and Blood.

Yeshua, Our Mighty Redeemer, with holy reverence, we remember and thank You for Your suffering on our behalf, which expunged our sin and redeemed our souls. And with grateful hearts we receive ALL of the KING-DOM benefits of Your holy sacrifice, which have brought us into our new identity in Christ and our new life of hope and victory. As we have Communion with Your Spirit, we ask you to forgive us and cleanse us from all unrighteousness and to build the resurrected Christ in us. **Jesus, You are the Bread of Life and the TREE of LIFE** (John 6:48). Therefore ...

WITH THIS BREAD, YOUR BODY:
We receive the power of Your abundant, eternal life abiding in us (John 6:50-51, 56 and 10:10). We receive all the fullness of Who You are, Christ in us, the hope of glory (Colossians 1:27). We eat healing power for our bodies and proclaim the finished work of the cross (John 19:30) to be effective in us to bring us Covenant wholeness. By Your stripes we are healed (Isaiah 53:4-5). **So, as we eat this bread, Lord, we partake of the TREE of LIFE and we thank You for Eternal, KINGDOM, Resurrection life through Your body** (John 6:48-51 and Revelation 5:12).

WITH THIS CUP OF THE NEW COVENANT IN YOUR BLOOD:
We drink and proclaim redemption for our souls. We drink the power of forgiveness and receive the release that it brings. We drink of the power that sets the captives free. We *declare complete victory over the enemy,* and we receive deliverance and cleansing from the guilt and power of sin and all of its destructive fruit, including sickness and disease (Hebrews 9:12-14). **And so we drink of the power of the Blood to seal our redemption, our healing, our protection and power to overcome every spiritual enemy. As we drink this cup, Lord, we thank You for the KINGDOM victory in Your Blood** (Revelation 12:11).

CELEBRATING COMMUNION TO HEAL AND CLEANSE THE LAND
(CELEBRATING THE TRIUMPH OF HIS KINGDOM, BEHOLDING HIS GLORY)

Worthy is the Lamb that was slain to receive power and riches and wisdom and strength and honor and glory and blessing!
Revelation 5:12

Jesus said, in John 6:48-58, that His body is REAL food and His Blood is REAL drink, and that as we receive His Body and Blood, we are receiving the very LIFE of GOD. Jesus also said that His Body was broken to bring **redemption and healing**, and His Blood was given to **cleanse** iniquity and to **seal** the New Covenant.

Although in the fullest understanding, Communion celebrates the Triumph of Christ and His Kingdom to restore all that was lost as a result of Adam's sin, what we are focusing on today is HEALING and REDEEMING **THE LAND** through the broken Body of Christ. Then we CLEANSE the land and SEAL it through His Blood of the New Covenant.

And so, Yeshua, Our Mighty Redeemer, we come with *holy reverence to this place.* We remember and thank You for Your suffering on our behalf which expunges all sin, death and defilement. And with grateful hearts we receive all of the restorative Kingdom benefits of Your holy sacrifice, for us and for this land.

Jesus, You are the Bread of LIFE and the Tree of LIFE (John 6:48).

As we partake of Your Body, the Bread of Life, we thank You for Eternal, Kingdom, Resurrection life. As we receive the life-giving and healing power of Your Body by faith, and as we commit a portion of Your Body to the land, we are extending to this land the power of Your abundant, eternal life. *We break all barrenness and all curses from the fall, and from the people who formerly occupied this land and who currently live here. We command this land to yield strength for every godly purpose. We declare that Jesus bore stripes, nails and thorns for the healing of this land and its inhabitants. We pray for revival, repentance, reconciliation and restoration.* As we celebrate the triumph of Your Kingdom in this place, we declare LIFE on this land, where death and darkness have prevailed. As we partake of your Body here, we thank You for Resurrection LIFE springing forth!

JESUS YOU ARE OUR VICTORY IN THE NEW COVENANT:

With this Cup of the New Covenant in Your Blood, we drink and proclaim redemption for our souls and for this land. We drink of the power that sets the captives free. As we receive and commit a portion of Your Blood to this land, we declare complete victory over the enemy, and we declare deliverance and cleansing from the guilt and power of sin and iniquity over us and over all people who have inhabited this land and the sin which has defiled it. *We break and cancel all blood covenants made on this land, and declare the land cleansed by the perfect blood of the Lamb of God and release the land from all demonic activity and curses.* As we drink this cup, Lord, we thank You for the KINGDOM victory in Your Blood (Revelation 12:11).[6]

---

6. The italicized words are from Dr. Bree Keyton, Bree Keyton Ministries.

CELEBRATING COMMUNION AS A PROPHETIC DECREE FOR LEADERS

(RECEIVING COMMUNION FOR OURSELVES AND, AS A PROPHETIC ACT, FOR OTHERS, ESPECIALLY THOSE IN PLACES OF GOVERNANCE)

CELEBRATING THE TRIUMPH OF HIS KINGDOM, BEHOLDING HIS GLORY:

Worthy is the Lamb that was slain to receive power and riches and wisdom and strength and honor and glory and blessing!

Revelation 5:12

Jesus said, in John 6:48-58, that His body is REAL food and His Blood is REAL drink, and that as we receive His Body and Blood, we are receiving the very LIFE of GOD, life that will never die. Jesus also said that His Body was broken for our Redemption and healing, and His Blood was given to cleanse iniquity and to seal the New Covenant.

Therefore, Yeshua, Our Mighty Redeemer, with *holy reverence* we remember and thank You for Your suffering on our behalf, which expunges all sin and defilement. And with grateful hearts we receive ALL of the restorative KINGDOM benefits of Your holy sacrifice for us and, *prophetically*, for our families, for our nation and for our governmental leaders.

As we have Communion with Your Spirit, we ask You to forgive us and cleanse us from all unrighteousness and to build the resurrected Christ in us:

HIS BODY: JESUS IS THE BREAD OF LIFE AND THE TREE OF LIFE (JOHN 6:48).

With this Bread, Yeshua's Body, we receive the power of His abundant, eternal life abiding in us (John 6:50-51, 56 and 10:10). We receive all the fullness of Who He is in us, *Christ, the hope of glory* (Colossians 1:27). We eat healing power for our bodies, our families, and for our nation and our governmental leaders. We proclaim the *finished work of the cross* (John 19:30) to be effective to bring *Covenant wholeness.* By His stripes all are healed — in our minds, bodies and spirits (Isaiah 53:4-5). As we celebrate the triumph of Your Kingdom, Lord, we declare LIFE and LIGHT everywhere that corruption, death and darkness have prevailed. And as we partake of Your body, we thank You for Resurrection LIFE springing forth (John 6:48-51 and Revelation 5:12).

HIS BLOOD — JESUS IS OUR VICTORY IN THE NEW COVENANT:
With this Cup of the New Covenant in Yeshua's Blood, we drink and proclaim redemption for our souls, for our families, for the nation and for our governmental leaders. We drink of the power that sets the captives free. We declare complete victory over the enemy, and we declare deliverance and cleansing from the guilt and power of sin, iniquity and deception over us and over our families, our nation and our leaders. And so we drink of the power of the Blood, to seal our redemption, our healing and the cleansing of this land and people from ALL defilement. **As we drink this cup, Lord, we thank You for the KINGDOM victory in Your Blood** (Revelation 12:11).

CHAPTER 10

PERSONAL AND DEVOTIONAL

DAILY PERSONAL LIFE DECLARATIONS

I command my day to fully cooperate with God's plan and purpose for it. All that I am and have belong to You, Lord. Use all for Your Glory. Thank You for perfecting that which concerns me (Psalm 138:8). Let the beauty of the Lord be upon me to establish the work of my hands (Psalm 90:17). Lord, fill me up and send me out with more love, more power and more of You in my life.

I declare that the Blood of Jesus has triumphed over and continues to prevail against all evil powers working to frustrate and interfere with my day, assignments, activities, my family, my relationships and my health. I have Covenant wholeness in mind, body and spirit (Isaiah 53:4-5). I shall flourish like a palm tree; I shall still bear fruit in old age; I shall be fresh and flourishing (Psalm 92:14).

I break all evil patterns, distractions, confusion and lies off the thoughts of my mind and bring every thought captive to the obedience of Christ (2 Corinthians 10:5). I resist the devil with the Blood of the Lamb, and he MUST flee from me (James 4:7)! I have the mind of Christ (1 Corinthians 2:16), and therefore I seek those things which are above and not the things beneath (Colossians 3:2). I receive the spiritual upgrading of my mind. I have sharp memory and recall. I WASH MY MIND IN THE BLOOD OF THE LAMB. I choose to set my mind on those things which are pure, lovely, just, virtuous, praiseworthy and of good report (Philippians 4:8). I commit my works to the Lord today, and my thoughts are established (Proverbs 16:3).

Father of Glory, unveil in me the riches of the Spirit of wisdom and of the Spirit of revelation through the fullness of being one with Christ, that the light of God would brighten the eyes of my innermost being, flooding me with light, until I experience the full revelation of our great hope of Glory (Ephesians 1:16-18a, *The Passion Translation*). Help me to know and embrace the Love of Christ which passes knowledge, that I might be filled with all the fullness of God (Ephesians 3:19).

TRUSTING GOD FOR GOOD IN THE FACE OF ADVERSITY

You saw who you created me to be before I became me!
Before I'd ever seen the light of day,
the number of days you planned for me
were already recorded in your book.

Psalm 139:14-16, The Passion Translation

I PROCLAIM THAT:

- God has planned every day of my life before I was even born (Psalm 139:14-16).
- My heritage is that no weapon forged against me will prevail, and I will refute every tongue that accuses me. This is my vindication from God (Isaiah 54:17).
- By Jesus' stripes, I am healed (Isaiah 53:5), and the Healer lives inside of me (Galatians 2:20).
- He who raised Christ from the dead will also give life to my mortal body (Romans 8:11).
- The Spirit also helps me in my weaknesses and makes intercession for me (Romans 8:26).
- God works all things out for my good as I love Him (Romans 8:28).
- I am more than a conqueror through Him who loves me (Romans 8:37).
- Nothing can separate me from the love of God (Romans 8:38-39).
- If God is for me, none can be against me (Romans 8:31).
- I am filled with the Lord of Glory. I am predestined, called, justified and glorified (Romans 8:28-30).

Lord Jesus, I trust You to complete the good work that You have begun in me, that I will fulfill my destiny in Christ that You planned out before I was even born (Philippians 1:6 and Psalm 139). The plans You have for me are plans for good, to give me hope and a sure future (Jeremiah 29:11). My Lord, work Your good pleasure in me, for Your Kingdom and Your Glory!

THE DAILY CONFESSIONS OF AN OVERCOMER

1. God is quickening me today to fulfill all that He has for me. I have a sure future because all His plans for me are for good, and He orders my steps according to His perfect will (1 Timothy 6:13, Jeremiah 29:11 and Psalm 37:23).

2. I am filled with power from on high and enabled to do exceedingly abundantly more than I could imagine, for He has prepared me to walk in the riches of His glory, and He surrounds me with His favor (Ephesians 3:20, Romans 9:23 and Psalm 5:12).

3. I have wholeness of mind, body and spirit because Jesus took upon Himself my sins and sicknesses on the cross of Calvary. And by His stripes I AM HEALED (Isaiah 53:4-5, Matthew 8:16-17 and 1 Peter 2:24).

4. God chooses to bless and prosper me and my finances in every way so that I can bless His children and fulfill my calling (Philippians 4:19 and 1 Chronicles 4:9-10).

5. I am more than a conqueror today through Jesus. His blood and my testimony cause me to triumph (Romans 8:37 and Revelation 12:11).

6. I have the mind of Christ, and so all I think and do is in agreement with His will. I have direction and focus because I hear His voice. I have no fear, for God has given me a sound mind, power and love. And Perfect love casts out all fear (1 Corinthians 2:16, John 10:4, 1 Timothy 1:7 and 1 John 4:18).

7. I can be at ease in the work He has given me to do because I have confidence that He will work through me, and I do not have to strive (Hebrews 4:9).

8. I am seated above circumstances with Christ in a place of protection and authority. There is no weapon formed against me that will prosper because I am in covenant with Almighty God, and all that He brings into my life is for my ultimate good and godliness (Ephesians 3:20, Luke 10:19, Isaiah 54:17, 1 Corinthians 11:25 and Romans 8:28).

PRAYING THE POWER OF THE RESURRECTION
(WITH AN UNDERSTANDING OF THE ORIGINAL GREEK AND INSIGHTS FROM ED CORLEY, *THE DYNAMICS OF CHRIST'S RESURRECTION*)

In Ephesians 1:19-22, Paul prayed that the Ephesians would know:

"... what is the exceeding greatness of His (1) power (dunamis) toward us who believe, according to the (2) working (energia) of His (3) mighty (ischuos) (4) power (kratos) which He (2) worked (energia) in Christ **when He raised Him from the dead and seated him at His right hand in the heavenly places** ... .

1. *Dunamis:* the force of creative miracles. This power removes obstacles and rearranges matter so that things not possible become realities. It releases souls from bondages and releases the abilities of the Holy Spirit.
2. *Energia:* dunamis harnessed and made productive. This power brings forth spirit life, makes effective the operation of the gifts of the Holy Spirit, and makes the life of a believer productive for the Kingdom of God.
3. *Ischuos:* the muscle power of deliverance. This power overcomes satanic strongholds and releases a person to be healed. It is the enabling power which gives believers strength to prevail in any demand or challenge coming against them.
4. *Kratos:* governmental power. This power reaches into the human heart once ruled by evil and sets up the new rule of Christ's Kingdom. It is the enabling that believers receive by the government of God resident within them.

KEY:

The **cross broke the power and guilt of sin** over our lives, but the **resurrection** affords us **the power and authority to live in** the victory of the cross. There are two directions in which the power of the Resurrection will work:

FOR DELIVERANCE OF THOSE WHO ARE BOUND:

"Gracious God, work in the hearts and minds of _____. Open their eyes that they may know the exceeding greatness of Your dynamic power unto "us who believe." May the *dunamis* and the *ischuos* power of Your Resurrection be fully manifested in their inner being, to uproot and destroy all satanic strongholds of sin, sickness, deception and emotional bondages. May Your *energia* power in them generate new life to bring them into the fullness of their destiny in God. As You pour Your Spirit and blessings upon them, we declare the *kratos* power of Your government is removing all carnal influences and that the government of their inner man is coming under the dominion of Christ and His Kingdom. Lord, give them the grace to receive what You will do in them. In their weakness, be their strength (*dunamis*) to overcome" (Ephesians 1:19-20, Isaiah 44:4-5 and 2 Corinthians 12:9).

FOR PERSONAL EMPOWERMENT TO LIVE AND MINISTER IN THE FULLNESS OF THE GOSPEL:

"Mighty God, may the fullness of the power of the Resurrection be manifested in my life. May Your *ischuos* muscle power deliver me from all that is carnal and unclean and empower me to prevail in and overcome every demand and challenge. May Your *dunamis* and *energia* power make effective the operation of the gifts of the spirit, with signs, wonders and miracles, that I might more effectively reveal Your Kingdom in this world. May the *kratos* power of Your government help me to be strong in the Lord and in the power of Your might. Establish the dominion of Your throne over my life, that I might live and minister as an overcomer in the full Resurrection power of the Gospel."

DECLARATIONS OF WHO
I AM IN CHRIST

"If One died for all, then all died; … Therefore, **if anyone is** *in Christ,* **he is a** *new creation***;** *old things have passed away; behold,* **all things have become new."** 2 Corinthians 5:14-17 (NLT)

"I am crucified with Christ; nevertheless I live, yet not I, **Christ lives** *in me."* Galatians 2:20

THEREFORE: I am *a new creature in Christ.* **My old nature** (with all of its negatives and failures) **is** *dead,* and **I am now alive to God** *in Christ,* **and HE** (with all of His goodness and victory) *is in me.* And so I am celebrating my NEW IDENTITY in Him!

1. My new life in Christ means that God does not see what is wrong with me (old man), but only what is missing in my experience that will upgrade me into the new person He sees in me.
2. Therefore, I am calling myself up to my new identity in Jesus because God only relates to my new man.
3. I am *transformed* by discovering who I am in Christ and behaving accordingly (Romans 12:2).
4. I am moving toward *advancement and destiny as I walk in newness of life in Christ.*
5. I am engaging with my new *identity,* not my circumstances. In Christ, I do not worry. *I trust.* I do not doubt. *I have faith* (Matthew 9:28-29 and Hebrews 11:1).
6. I cannot fail because all the "issues" of my life are *in Christ* because *I am in Christ,* and God has predetermined the outcome (Jeremiah 29:11).
7. I can do all things through Christ Who strengthens me *from within* (Philippians 4:13).
8. As He is, so am I in this world (1 John 4:17) — beautiful, powerful, anointed, prophetic, wise, strong, overcoming and victorious.

9. I am a *habitation* for the Lord, living under a *weight of majesty* (1 Corinthians 6:19-20 and John 14:21 and 23).

10. Therefore, I choose a *triumphal* life perspective and see victory in every situation. I am fighting *from a place of victory*, not toward it (Ephesians 2:6 and 1 John 3:8).

11. I am *more than a conqueror* because of my *identity in Christ*. Jesus has overcome, so *I overcome* — so that the devil cannot touch me (Romans 8:37 and 1 John 5:4-5 and 18).

12. I am *renewed daily* in the spirit of my mind, putting on the new man (new identity), which is created by God in true righteousness and holiness (Ephesians 4:24).

13. I have the mind of Christ (1 Corinthians 2:16), which *is always positive, joyfully confident, thinking brilliantly and full of life and peace.*

14. I am subject to *refreshing, as rivers of living waters* flow out of me (John 7:38).

15. I am *passionately abiding* in faith in Christ and filled with *expectation and hope* (Colossians 1:27).

16. I am confident in God's *love and goodness* toward me (Psalm 52:1 and John 3:16).

17. I am ruled by the *goodness of God*. My blessings are stored up in heaven and are being released into my life (Psalm 68:19).

18. *I am an overcomer* as I take pleasure in the goodness of God (Romans 8:37-39).

19. I am *beloved by God*. My Father delights in me (Psalm 18:19).

20. I continue to ask, knowing I will receive, because *my Father loves to bless me* (Matthew 7:7-11).

21. I am learning the new vocabulary of the *overcoming life* I have in Christ (John 16:33).

22. I am being *strengthened in my faith* through all my life's circumstances (Hebrews 12:2).

23. I am *counting it all joy* because God is causing me to triumph in every situation (James 1:2 and 1 Corinthians 15:57).

24. I cannot be shaken because I belong to a Kingdom which cannot be shaken (Hebrews12:28).

25. I choose to be controlled by *the Spirit of God* (in my circumstances) and *not* controlled by my circumstances.

26. I do not focus on the negative or the problem, but I pray for the *positive replacement*. This is how I turn every negative into a positive and learn to prosper through every circumstance.

27. I am a joint heir with Christ. It is *my birthright to live in Divine advantage* (favor)(Romans 8:16-17).

28. I am established in Christ in *favor and promise*. I am a magnet for *blessing, favor and upgrade* because of Jesus in me (Colossians 1:27).

29. I believe, choose and expect *favor* until circumstances become favorable (Psalm 5:12).

30. I am alive to God and living with Him (Romans 8:8 and 11).

31. I am living an *ascended lifestyle*. God is not dealing with my sin; He is *establishing my righteousness* (2 Corinthians 5:21).

32. As I abide in Christ, I walk in *resurrection power* (Romans 8:11).

33. I am living in the *unforced rhythms of outrageous grace*. I am well content in Grace (Ephesians 2:2).

34. The majesty of Grace is that it is inexhaustible. Grace is working in me through the Holy Spirit to empower me to become the person God sees in me (John 14:16-17).

35. **My testimony of Grace is this:** "I am what I am by the Grace of God" and because I AM lives in me.

SUMMARY DECLARATION FOR DAILY PRAYER:

As Jesus is, so am I in this world (1 John 4:17) — beautiful, powerful, anointed, prophetic, wise, strong, overcoming, victorious – at ONE with the Father (John 14:23). I have the mind of Christ (1 Corinthians 2:16), which is always positive, joyfully confident, thinking brilliantly and full of life and peace. It is my birthright to live in Divine favor (Psalm 5:12). I do not live under any circumstances. I am seated with Christ in heavenly places (Ephesians 2:6), and I am learning how to live *heaven to earth*. I choose to be challenged by God and not my problems. Therefore, I am joyfully vulnerable to God's ability in the midst of my difficulties. I am looking beyond my circumstances to see who God wants to be for me in every situation. I turn every negative into a positive by praying for the positive replacement instead of focusing on the problem. This is how I learn to prosper through every circumstance and how I use my problems to bring empowerment and upgrade into my life. I am living an ascended lifestyle, and God is establishing my righteousness. Grace is empowering me to become the person God sees in me. Therefore, I am advancing toward upgrade and destiny.

Awaken my heart, Lord. Open my eyes to all that You are, all that I am in You, and everything we can be together. "*O surpassing greatness of the indwelling power of God, rise up and transform me, transfigure me, beautify me until my face shines with Your glory. Change me from glory to glory* (2 Corinthians 3:18) *until I have an **unbreakable spirit** and **unshakable faith!***"[7]

---

7. Italicized words by Julia C. Loren. Identify statements compiled with insights from Graham Cooke.

DECLARATION OVER MY MIND

I declare that I am a **new creature** *in Christ* - my old ways of thinking and doing have passed away - and all is NEW (2 Corinthians 5:17)!

I receive **renewal in the spirit of my mind** as I put on my new *holy and righteous character* created in me by my heavenly Father (Ephesians 4:23-24).

I declare that the **Blood of Jesus** has triumphed over and continues to prevail against the enemy of my soul who is working to frustrate my day and my destiny in the battleground of my mind (Colossians 2:15). I resist the devil, and he must flee from me (James 4:7)!

As I confess my sin and wash my mind in the **Blood of Jesus** today, I receive its *purifying and life-giving properties* in my thought life (Isaiah 53:5 and 1 John 1:9).

I pull down every stronghold and break every evil pattern, distraction, lies and confusion off of the thoughts of my mind (2 Corinthians 10:4), and *bring every thought captive into obedience to Christ* (2 Corinthians 10:5).

I set my mind on things **above** and not things on the earth (Colossians 3:2).

I have **perfect peace** because I keep my mind focused on *God* and not my problems (Isaiah 26:3).

I am not fearful or anxious because God has given me a **sound mind,** power and love (2 Timothy 1:7). **And perfect love casts out all fear** (1 John 4:17).

I therefore *choose* not to be anxious about anything, but to bring my needs to God in prayer and *trust* that He will work everything out for my good. (Philippians 4:6 and Romans 8:28).

As I have freely receive **forgiveness** from God, I freely give forgiveness to all who have wronged me. As I do this, *my mind is set free to receive all that God has for me* (Ephesians 4:32).

I have received the Spirit Who is from God, that I might know the things that are freely given to me by God. **I have the mind of Christ** (1 Corinthians 2:12 and 16).

I receive in my mind *a Spirit of wisdom and revelation in the knowledge of God* (Ephesians 4:7 and 9).

I choose to set my mind on these things: **whatsoever things are noble, just, pure, lovely, virtuous, praiseworthy and of good report** (Philippians 4:8). As I dwell on these things, the *God of Peace will continue to guard my heart and mind through Christ Jesus* (Philippians 4:7 and 9).

A PERSONAL DECLARATION OF FAITH AND DEDICATION

Gracious Father, I come before You in the Name of Your precious Son, Jesus, Who by His atoning and sacrificial death, made the way for me to enter with boldness to Your throne of Grace to find help in my time of need (Hebrews 4:12). Jesus, with the pouring out of His blood, cleansed me from all my sin, taking sinfulness and the law which condemned me and nailing it to the cross (Colossians 2:14), so that I might have the righteousness of God through Him (2 Corinthians 5:21). On this Rock I stand — upon no other foundation will I build (1 Corinthians 3:11).

The seat of authority in my heart is possessed by the King of kings and Lord of lords (Revelation 19:16). I live to function as a conduit (John 4:14) of Your love to a lost and dying world. I put on the Lord Jesus Christ (Romans 13:14), and put to death my flesh, my self, that the light and life and love of Jesus might flow through me (Galatians 2:20), and that that light may so shine before men as to continually bring You glory through the good works that I do (Matthew 5:16).

I pray that Your Son, Jesus, may be glorified in and through me, and that as I pray in His name and in perfect unity with His will, whatever I ask, You will grant it unto me (John 16:23). According as IT IS WRITTEN, I believe, therefore I speak … (2 Corinthians 4:13 and Psalm 116:10). And whatever things I desire, when I pray, believing, I shall have them (Mark 11:24).

KINGDOM IDENTITY DECLARATIONS

Holy Spirit, I declare my allegiance to Your work and power within me to bring me into the fullness of who I **am IN Christ, as a son of God in the Kingdom** (Romans 8:19 – positioning, not gender). And I deny all works, influences and passions of the flesh that try to keep me in bondage to the old man I used to be.

This is my **declaration toward upgrade** as a son of God:

I am a son of God, lead by the Spirit of God. Because the Spirit of God dwells in me, I am alive to Christ, and my flesh does not rule over me. I am Spirit-led and not flesh-driven. The Holy Spirit Who raised Christ from the dead continually quickens my mortal body to become a resurrected body. As I abide in His Presence, saturated with His Glory, I am filled with His vigorous life. I continually feed on things that have spiritual and Kingdom substance, so I can reveal His Glory and His Kingdom in the earth as it is in Heaven (Romans 8:10, 2 and 11).

For — "My **citizenship is in heaven**, from which I also eagerly wait for the Savior, the Lord Jesus Christ, Who will **transform (transfigure) my lowly body that it may be conformed to His glorious body …**" (Philippians 3:20-21). I become whatever I set my eyes upon. Therefore, as I behold the Glory of the Lord with unveiled face, **I am being changed into the same image from glory to glory** (2 Corinthians 3:18). And as I have received the first fruits of the Spirit, I inwardly groan and passionately long to experience my physical body being transformed. This is my **full status of sonship** (Romans 8:23, *The Passion Translation*). Because the cross defeated the curse that came as a result of Adam's sin, I am opened to a **whole new realm of living**. "Jesus is the Savior Who brings the Kingdom realm to all who believe" (Galatians 3:22).

Therefore, I AM:

- Not subject to the curse of sin and death, but subject to the **Spirit of Abundant LIFE** in Christ Jesus (Galatians 3:13, Romans 8:2 and John 5:24 and 10:10).
- Not a "human being," but a **spiritual being,** created in the image of God (Romans 8:3-24).
- An **Overcomer over this natural realm** and not subject to the physical laws of this world (John 16:33, Revelation 3:21 and John 14:12).
- Created to live as the **connector between the spiritual and natural worlds**, able to interface with both realms at the same time (John 1:51).
- Filled with **creative light** (the Light of the world lives in me) which is reprogramming my DNA to become a resurrected body (John 1:9, 8:12 and Philippians 3:20).

THEREFORE, BECAUSE OF MY POSITION OF BEING **ONE** WITH CHRIST, AND MY POSITION OF AUTHORITY AS A JOINT-HEIR WITH HIM:

- Everything Jesus has *is mine* (and everything I have is His).
- Everywhere He is *I am* (and everywhere I am He is).
- Everything He does *I can do.*
- All that He is *I can be* (not Divinity, but the fruitful *character* of Divinity: "Christ in me the hope of Glory" (Ephesians 2:6, John 14:12, 20, Romans 8:16-17, 1 John 4:17, Colossians 1:27 and Galatians 5:22-23).

OFFERING YOURSELF AS A LIVING SACRIFICE

*I beseech you therefore, brethren, by the mercies of God, **that you present your bodies a living sacrifice, holy, acceptable to God**, which is my spiritual act of worship.*   Romans 12:1

Hebraically, this is how the high priest would sacrifice the lamb:

1. First, he would confess the sin over the lamb.
2. Next, he would cut the throat and drain the blood. The life is in the blood, and the lamb, just like Jesus, was conceived for the purpose of sacrifice.
3. He would skin it. Skin is the container of life, the covering of flesh.
4. He would cut it open and take the insides out, cleaning out the inside of the body
5. He would then cut the head off. The head represents government, surrendering the government of the body to the government of God.
6. Then, the legs, representing the walk or style of life, would be cut off. This is surrendering your life.
7. Finally, he cut through the sternum and backbone to open the whole lamb and lay it bare, so that nothing was hidden from the priest's gaze.

APPLYING THE HEBREW PROTOCOL TO OFFER YOURSELF AS A LIVING SACRIFICE:

This is spiritual imagery in a realm that is accessed by faith. Ours is a living and a spiritual sacrifice, modeled after the offering of the Hebraic sacrificial lamb.

... having boldness to enter the holiest by the Blood of Jesus, by a new and living way which He consecrated for us, through the veil, that is His flesh ...   Hebrews 10:19-20

PRESENTATION TO YESHUA, THE HIGH PRIEST:

My purpose is to live a lifestyle of engagement with the Kingdom/ Presence of God. Therefore, I come to **"present my body a living sacrifice, holy, acceptable to God**, which is my spiritual act of worship." (Romans 12:1) — To do this by FAITH…

1. **I take a step forward through the veil** (Hebrews10:19-20, above), **out of Time (where I live) and into Eternity (where God lives)** and *host my body as a spirit being into the presence of God.*

2. **And I present my body (Romans 12:1) to Yeshua, my High Priest** … . My body is Your temple, Yeshua. **I surrender my life into the realm of Your Presence today.** I give you the coverings of my body and ask You to skin me. Take every false covering that has kept me hidden from the realm of Your Presence.

3. **My High Priest, take the Word of God, which is sharper than a double-edged sword, and cut open my inner being** (Hebrews 4:12). Take the deep-rooted things inside my life that hurt Your heart. I expose all my inner man, every internal organ, to Your cleansing of everything that defiles. Create in me a clean heart and put a right spirit within me, that the words of my mouth and the meditations of my heart would be acceptable in Your sight, O Lord, my strength and my Redeemer (Psalms 51:10 and 19:14). *Thank You for bringing my life into Your Divine order and my Divine destiny.*

4. **I surrender my head, and give you the work of Government in my body.** *I declare that the ruling authority of God's Kingdom is established over and governs my life.*

5. **I surrender my arms and legs, my walk and lifestyle,** to You, My High Priest. *I declare my steps are ordered by the Lord.*

6. **I present myself as a living sacrifice in the Kingdom world of my Father.**

7. **I position myself to receive all that is available to me in the Kingdom supply of My Father,** so that I might rule on earth as a

son of the Kingdom (Romans 8:19). I receive the impartation of **the garment of holiness** (Joshua in Zechariah 3).

8. Thank You, Yeshua, that You have made me *holy and whole.* Through Your precious Blood, I am *acceptable* in Your sight. The power of the cross has canceled every curse that came as a result of Adam's sin. I am now subject to the **Spirit of life in Christ Jesus.** Holy Spirit, help me to appropriate Christ-likeness in thought, word and deed. *Christ in me is the Hope of Glory* (Colossians 1:27).

9. **I wrap my body back up and put the pieces back together with the Presence of the Glory of God woven into the fabric of who I am,** so that I would shine with the very Radiance of Your Glory (Isaiah 60:1 and 5).

I bring my body back out into this world, stepping out of Eternity and back into Time. Abba, thank You that I am acceptable, holy and made whole, because my body is Your temple. Empower me to become **a reflection of Your Kingdom** here on earth as it is in Heaven. Help me to **engage who I am as a *son* of God** (position, not gender, Romans 8:18-19), reflecting the fullness of Christ, bringing me into **full sonship** in the Kingdom, so I might live **a lifestyle of engagement** with the Kingdom/Presence of God. [8]

---

8. With gleanings from Ian Clayton (www.sonofthunder.org).

LIFE DECLARATIONS

- Let Your kingdom come and Your will be done in my life as it is in heaven.
- I am walking in the timing of the Lord.
- I live to function and conduct my life's affairs according to your original plan and purpose. Send Your gathering Angels to extract the tares from my life (Matthew 13:41).
- I command my day to fully cooperate with Your plan and purpose for it. All that I am and have belong to You. Use it for Your Glory. Thank You for perfecting that which concerns me (Psalm 138:8). Let the beauty of the Lord be upon me to establish the work of my hands (Psalm 90:17). Lord, fill me up and send me out with more love, more power, more of You.
- The Blood of Jesus has triumphed over and continues to prevail against evil powers working to frustrate and interfere with my day, assignments, activities, my family, my health and my relationships.
- I break evil patterns, distractions, confusion and lies off the thoughts of my mind and bring every thought captive to the obedience of Christ (2 Corinthians 10:5). I resist the devil, and he MUST flee from me!
- *I have the mind of Christ,* and therefore I seek those things which are above and not the things beneath. I receive the spiritual upgrading of my mind. I have sharp memory and recall. I WASH MY MIND IN THE BLOOD OF THE LAMB. I choose to set my mind on those things which are pure, lovely, just, virtuous, praiseworthy and of good report (Philippians 4:8).
- *I have Covenant wholeness* in mind, body and spirit (Isaiah 53:4-5). I shall be fresh and flourishing and fruit-bearing even in my old age (Psalm 92:14).
- I commit my works to the Lord, and my thoughts are established (Proverbs 16:3), because my mind is illuminated with the Light of Revelation!

REJOICING IN ALL I HAVE IN CHRIST

This is the day the Lord has made;
I will REJOICE and be glad in it!   Psalm 118:24

My joy is not based on my circumstances, but on **Who God is for me.**

Therefore, I CHOOSE today to REJOICE because:

- God's goodness and compassion are new every morning (Lamentations 3:21-23).
- Nothing can separate me from the Love of God! I am His Beloved (Romans 8:39).
- Jesus loved me so much that He died for me! (John 3:16 and Mark 10:45).
- I am redeemed (Galatians 3:13) and sanctified (Hebrews 10:10) by the Blood of Jesus.
- My God will never leave me or forsake me (Hebrews 13:15).
- God's favor surrounds me like a shield (Psalm 5:12).
- God's perfect love casts out all fear in my life! (1 John 4:18).
- His GRACE is sufficient for me, for in my weakness He is STRONG (2 Corinthians 12:9).
- Father above has given me every good and perfect gift (1 Corinthians 12 and James 1:17).
- Father's plans for me are for a future of hope, success and joy (Jeremiah 29:11, John 15:11 and 17:13).
- His power has given me ALL THINGS I need to have a prosperous and God-honoring life (2 Peter 1:3).
- Jesus is IN ME (Galatians 2:20), and I am IN HIM (2 Corinthians 5:17).
- Jesus took my old life of sin and gave me His righteousness (2 Corinthians 7:21).
- I have been set free from the law of sin and death (Romans 8:2).

- I am more than a conqueror (Romans 8:37), and no weapon formed against me shall prosper (Isaiah 54:17).
- I am seated with Christ in heavenly places of victory (Ephesians 2:6 and Colossians 2:15).
- Jesus has overcome, so I overcome (John 16:33 and Revelation 12:11).
- I have the mind of Christ (1 Corinthians 2:16).
- I can do all things through Christ Who strengthens me (Philippians 4:13).
- My God shall supply all my needs (Philippians 4:19).
- God's angel-guard of deliverance is encamped around me (Psalm 34:7).
- I have wholeness of mind, body and spirit because Jesus took upon Himself my sins and sicknesses on the cross of Calvary. And *by His stripes I am healed* (Isaiah 53:4-5, Matthew 8:16-17 and 1 Peter 2:24).

REJOICE in the Lord always, and again I say REJOICE!

Philippians 4:4

MY PROCLAMATION OF LOVE TO HIM
(FROM DAVID'S PSALMS AND THE SONG OF SOLOMON)

YOU ARE MY MAGNIFICENT OBSESSION:

My soul magnifies the LORD and my spirit has rejoiced in God my Savior.   Luke 1:46-47

You are fairer than the sons of men; grace is poured upon Your lips.
Psalm 45:2

You are the awesome LORD Most High, the great King over all the earth.
Psalm 47:2

My eyes are upon You, O God, my LORD.   Psalm 141:8

My heart says to You: Your face, Lord, will I seek.   Psalm 27:8

Oh God, You are my God, early will I seek You. My soul thirsts for You; my flesh longs for you.   Psalm 63:1

Your love is better than wine; draw me away.
Song of Solomon 1:2 and 4

Behold, You are handsome, My Beloved – Yes, pleasant!
Song of Solomon 1:16

You are like an apple tree among the trees of the woods. I long to sit in Your shade and eat of Your sweet fruit.   Song of Solomon 2:3

I long to sit with You at Your banqueting table under Your banner of love.   Song of Solomon 2:4

Sustain me ... refresh me ... for I am lovesick for You.
Song of Solomon 2:5

By night on my bed I seek You, the ONE I love.
Song of Solomon 3:1

You are chief among 10,000. Song of Solomon 5:10

You are altogether lovely ... my Beloved ... my Friend.
Song of Solomon 5:16

Set me as a seal upon Your heart; as a seal upon Your arm – consume me with Your love. Song of Solomon 8:6

Come, my Beloved, let us get up early to the vineyards to enjoy the pleasant fruits ... there I will give You my love.
Song of Solomon 7:12-13

I am my Beloved's and my Beloved is mine – and His desire is toward me. Song of Solomon 7:10

OH, TO LOVE HIM MORE!

*You shall love the Lord your God with **all** your heart, with **all** your soul,
and with **all** your mind. This is the first and greatest commandment. "*
Matthew 22:37-38

One day, as I was meditating on this commandment during my devotional-worship time, I was deeply convicted of the deficiency and imperfection of my love for the Lord. I wrote in my journal that with this conviction came the awareness of the transcending importance of such love from the Bride to the Bridegroom. My heart cry was that although He had supplied all my needs, there was one need I still had: **That I would love Him more.** I wrote from my contrite heart:

My heart calls to You in the early morn;
   my soul is longing to meet Thee.
Thirsty and hungry I sit at Your feet,
Lord, fill me again, I beseech Thee,
   For I need to love Thee more.
My soul is forgiven, cleansed and renewed,
   as on wings of an eagle I soar.
With power from Heaven is my spirit endued,
   my sins condemn me no more.
   Yet I would love thee more.
Lifted into the heavenly realm,
   by your Spirit I draw near.
Into Your Presence, embraced by your love,
   I have no need nor fear,
   But only to love Thee more.
Lovingly, gently You guide my steps,
   as I trust You with all my heart,
   strengthening me at every turn,
   and though faith You do impart.

I yearn to love Thee more.
As I lay down in peace at the close of the day,
   knowing the angels their vigil do keep,
   I pray to my God who comforts me,
   and gives His beloved sleep:
Lord, help me to love thee more.

MY KETUBAH
(THE *KETUBAH* IS A HEBREW MARRIAGE CONTRACT DATING BACK TO ANCIENT TIMES. THE LITERAL TRANSLATION OF *KETUBAH* IS "IT IS WRITTEN." MY *KETUBAH* BELOW (WHICH I SHARE AS AN EXAMPLE) IS FRAMED *OUT OF SCRIPTURE*, LITERALLY "IT IS WRITTEN"

WHAT I DESIRE TO RECEIVE
(HE HAS PREPARED A DESTINY FOR ME TO WALK IN):

- I choose Your Name over great riches to be my very own (Proverbs 22:1).
- I desire for You to spread Your wing over me and enter into covenant with me and make me Yours, and that You would wash me and clothe me with a pure and beautiful wedding garment (Ezekiel 16:8-10 and Revelation 19:8).
- I desire that You would break the seal and open my Testimony Scroll, to release my destiny that You purposed in Your heart before I was formed in my mother's womb (Psalm 139:15-18 and Jeremiah 29:11).
- I desire that You would tune my senses to heaven so I can commune with You in the heavenly realms with the fellowship we had before the foundation of the world. Bring me in remembrance of what we had together (Jeremiah 1:5).
- I desire to move freely between earth and heaven on the stairway that You spoke to Nathaniel about (John 1:50-52), and that I would see You face to face as Moses did (Genesis 32:30).
- I desire to receive from You wisdom, knowledge and understanding, so that I might impart Truth that would liberate and empower people to live in their full potential and destiny in Christ, so as to advance the Kingdom on earth as it is in heaven (Proverbs 4:5-9, 10:13-14 and Matthew 6:10).
- I desire that You would change the record and frequency in my body's DNA to become a shadow that Your Creative Light can sit on, so that I may become a Resurrection, Creative Light being like You,

fully manifesting the image of God on the earth (Genesis 1:26-27).

- I desire to walk with You in the cool of the day along the River of Life (Genesis 3:8 and Revelation 22:1-2).
- I desire to live in the Magnificent Radiance of Your Glory forever (Psalm 26:8).

WHAT I DESIRE TO GIVE WITH THE HELP OF THE HOLY SPIRIT (HE REQUIRES OF ME MY TOTAL LOVE, DEVOTION AND TRUST):

- I want to be Your Treasured Possession and Your daily delight (Proverbs 8:1).
- I want to cleave to You, abide with You and love You with all my heart, soul, mind and strength (John 15:4-7 and Mark 12:30).
- I desire to so live the Truth that my life and words will compel others to follow You (John 14:6).
- I desire that our union would bring forth much fruit to Your glory, and that this fruit would be a lasting and pure reflection of the image of God on the earth (John 15:8 and Matthew 5:16).
- I desire for You to receive a hundredfold increase on Your investment in me. I desire to be in the Holy of Holies (Psalm 26:8 and 27:4).
- I desire to walk with You as Enoch did, in the power of perfect love and intimacy with You (Genesis 5:24).
- I purpose to deny myself, take up my cross, and follow You wherever You lead me (Matthew 16:24).
- I purpose to take You at Your Word and to completely trust You in Your absolute goodness and love for me in all things, regardless of the circumstances (Proverbs 3:5-6).
- I desire to have such a grateful heart that all that is within me would continuously be praising Your Holy Name (Psalm 103:1-2).
- I desire to live my life so close to You that You take pleasure in my every prayer (Psalm 27:46, The Passion Translation).
- I desire to be an Overcomer so that I can sit with You on Your throne (Revelation 3:21).

PRAISE THE LORD!

Let everything that has breath praise the LORD!   Psalm 150

You, O Lord, are a God full of compassion, and gracious, longsuffering and abundant in mercy and truth.   Psalm 86:15

You are:

OMNISCIENT – ALL KNOWING

OMNIPOTENT – ALL POWERFUL

OMNIPRESENT – ALL PRESENT

How I praise You:

For Your excellent GREATNESS. There is NONE like YOU!

For Your radiant GLORY that fills the heavens!

For Your everlasting, unchangeable, immeasurable LOVE!

For Your indescribable BEAUTY displayed in Creation!

For Your enduring MERCIES that are new every morning!

For Your perfect JUSTICE executed in the earth!

For Your abounding GRACE that causes us to Overcome!

For Your unfathomable WISDOM extended to all!

For Your unfailing COMPASSION that sees beyond my sin!

For Your enduring SHALOM that subdues chaos!

Great is the Lord and greatly to be praised!   Psalm 48:1

EPILOGUE

I would like to close this book with some KINGDOM thoughts:

God's **Kingdom** is where His government rules and His supernatural life is manifested.

In Matthew 13:11, Jesus said: "It *has been given to you to know the mysteries of the Kingdom.*" Jesus personified the Kingdom. He spoke the Kingdom, He lived the Kingdom, and He demonstrated what life in the Kingdom should be like. For a number of years now I have been on a journey of discovery about who we are and what we have in Christ *and how we are to manifest and proclaim the Kingdom as Jesus did.* The truth is: because the cross defeated the curse that came as a result of Adam's sin, we are opened to a whole new realm of living! Galatians 3:22 tells us:

"Jesus is the Savior who brings the Kingdom realm to all who believe."

I would like to share a little Kingdom analogy that has flowed out of my experience of walking in and declaring Kingdom realities:

My husband and I love to hike. When you are hiking in mountain country, sometimes there is a long hike just to get to the foot of a mountain. This hike along the trail to the mountain affords you a beautiful, yet limited, view. Then, as you are making the ascent, you are so focused on where to place your foot that you only see what is directly ahead of you. When you finally reach the summit and turn around to see from whence you have come, it takes your breath away. A whole new vista is opened up to you that was there all the time, but you just couldn't see it from your earthbound vantage point.

This is life in the Spirit that reveals the Kingdom! I feel like most of my life I have been hiking along the valley, and now I am climbing the mountain. I am not talking about having a "mountain-top" experience in the traditional sense. **I am talking about gaining a *Kingdom perspective* that lifts you out of the natural and into the supernatural, out of time and into eternity, out of limitation and into "nothing is impossible."**

This is how Jesus lived on earth. And since Jesus, the Creator of all that is, lives inside of us, should we expect anything less?

As Paul reminds us in the letter to the Colossians:

*Christ's resurrection from the dead is your resurrection too. This is why we are to yearn for all that is **above**, for that's where Christ sits **enthroned at the place of all power; honor; and authority**! Yes, feast on all the treasures of the heavenly realm and fill your thoughts with heavenly realities, and not with the distractions of the natural realm. Your crucifixion with Christ has severed the tie to this life, and now your true life is hidden away in God as you live **within the Anointed One** ... . And every time Christ Himself is seen for Who He really is, who you really are will also be revealed, for you are now **one with Him in His glory**!* Colossians 3:1-5, The Passion Translation

Seated with Christ in heavenly places, at one with Him in His Glory, declaring HIS KINGDOM COME AND HIS WILL BE DONE. That is to be our life in the Spirit.

*This is how we proclaim Heaven to Earth prayers. This is how we are going to demonstrate the Kingdom of Power and Light against the increasing darkness that is coming upon the world in these last days. Only a **supernaturally-living and speaking people** can accurately reflect the image of a supernatural God and bring **the reality of the life of His eternal Kingdom here on earth — now — as it is in Heaven**.*

On July 27, 2017 I was hiking at 12,000 feet in the Colorado Rockies. As I positioned myself on a rock outcropping in the alpine tundra, silence, peace and beauty overwhelmed me. I soaked in the scene of distant, majestic, snow-capped mountain peaks and miniature flowers on pin cushions of soft, green moss at my feet. What a glorious landscape! What a glorious Creator! As my worship flowed up to Heaven, the Lord spoke:

My Kingdom is rising as My Ekklesia takes its position. My Glory — not just the knowledge of it, but My GLORY — shall cover the earth as the waters cover the sea. Time is short, but My purposes will be fulfilled. I alone am God. I will NOT be denied. ALL nations shall come and worship Me. EVERY knee shall bow before My Son, whom I have exalted as Supreme Judge of the Universe – King of kings and Lord of lords. Wherever His name is lifted up, My Glory shall fall. Hold tightly to Me as the kingdoms of this world begin to crumble and collapse. Only Mine shall remain, and it shall be GLORIOUS!

Made in the USA
Columbia, SC
11 December 2020